THE HERMITAGE
ESSAYS ON THE HISTORY
OF THE COLLECTION

OLEG NEVEROV, MIKHAIL PIOTROVSKY

THE HERMITAGE

ESSAYS ON THE HISTORY
OF THE COLLECTION

SLAVIA
ART BOOKS

St Petersburg

Eduard Hau (1807 – about 1870).
Gallery of 1812. 1862. Watercolour.
43.9 × 31 cm. The Hermitage

Coptic fabric. 4th century. Egypt.
Cotton, linen, wool. Diam. 25.5 cm.
The Hermitage.
Bought by Vladimir Bock

*Texts by **Oleg Neverov** and **Mikhail Piotrovsky***
*Translated from the Russian by **Inna Sorokina***
*Designed by **Luca Selmi***
*Photographs by **Vladimir Terebenin** and **Leonard Kheifets***
*Edited by **Ninel Mikhaliova***

ISBN 5-88654-026-1

Contents

This volume is devoted to one of the world's major art museums and the people who amassed its celebrated collections: Russian nobles, diplomats, members of the museum staff, Fiodor Bruni and Stepan Gedeonov (the former directors of the Hermitage), and such enthusiasts as Nikolai Likhachov and Alexander Basilewsky, who donated their treasures to the Museum. The volume surveys the archaeological excavations of Scythian barrows, the town of Nymphaeum, the Altaic burial grounds of Pazyryk, the Urartian stronghold of Karmir-Blur, and Pianjikent. It highlights the activities of the Stroganov and Sheremetev families and tells how their collections found their way to the Hermitage after the 1917 revolution. The author dwells on the Oriental collection built by the outstanding scholar Joseph Orbeli and on the redistribution of art works between the Hermitage and other museums in the post-revolutionary years, paying particular attention to the history of the Morozov and Shchukin collections. A special account is devoted to the Hermitage staff's efforts to preserve the collections during the world wars and at a time when there was a tendency to sell works of art abroad or to transfer them to provincial museums. The book also gives information on recent acquisitions made by the Hermitage Purchasing Commission, on generous gifts of the friends of the Museum, and on Peter the Great's palaces uncovered on the Hermitage premises.

Mikhail Piotrovsky,
Director of the Hermitage

18th Century

Alexander Ziablov (d. 1784). Picture
Gallery of Ivan Shuvalov (Copy of
Fiodor Rokotov's painting). About
1757. Oil on canvas. History
Museum, Moscow

Casket with scenes of The Fall.
16th century. Spain. Ivory, wood.
20.5 × 15 cm. The Hermitage. From
the Kunstkammer collection

It is believed that the casket with scenes
of the Fall was produced in Ceylon.
In 1716, Peter the Great purchased it
from the Dutch apothecary, Albert Seba.
The casket contained Oriental ornaments:
wild boar's fangs mounted in gold,
antlers and hoofs of Guinea stags, etc.

10

Catherine the Great, Founder of the Hermitage

The foundation of the Hermitage is traditionally referred to the year 1764 when an important collection of paintings was acquired from Johann Ernest Gotzkowski. As far as the history of the picture gallery in the Winter Palace is concerned, this dating is perfectly correct. Yet the roots of the Hermitage as a cultural history museum reach farther back into the past — to the reign of Peter the Great. Peter's interests as collector were not centred on paintings alone. His *Kunstkammer*, the first public museum in Russia, had a universal character, as did his private collections. In particular, it had, from its inception, an archaeological section containing findings from native sites, although obtained in an irregular way, as a result of clandestine diggings by treasure hunters. The artifacts came from the vast and fabulously rich land of Siberia, a region on which were pinned the country's hopes of a new rise to greatness.

In 1715, one of Siberia's pioneer industrialists, Akinfy Nikitich Demidov, whose activity in exploiting the natural resources of the land served not only his own interests but also those of the Crown, presented to Catherine Alexeyevna, Peter's wife, a splendid gift on the occasion of the birth of an heir. The gift consisted of twenty gold art objects of most curious design and mysterious nature. This series of magnificent ornaments formed only a small fraction of the boundless wealth extracted annually by the grave-diggers of the Urals and Siberia from the tall burial mounds left behind by the ancient inhabitants of the land, the Scythians, Sauromatae, Sakae, and other carriers of the once flourishing culture of the Eurasian steppes.

This kind of clandestine digging was widely practised in Siberia. To some it was a profession; to others, a seasonal occupation. The gold artifacts from the burial mounds were sold or melted down as soon as found. Ancient cultural remains were fast disappearing. Even the very first scientific expeditions which hastened to the region in the early 18th century, closely following in the tracks of

the treasure hunters, found but little gold. Those that went after them found still less.

It was by acting with his usual promptitude that Peter unwittingly salvaged for the science not a few objects quite unique in their artistic and archaeological value. Struck by the brilliance and beauty of the Scythian buckles and plaques, the Tsar, who had caught some of the passion for archaeology from European sovereigns during his travels, at once gave Matvei Gagarin, Governor of Siberia, strict injunctions that all antiquities derived from local burial mounds should be collected and sent to St Petersburg. His orders were obeyed. In the following year, the first lot of gold artifacts arrived in the capital.

Placed in the *Kunstkammer*, they formed the basis of what is known as Peter the Great's Siberian Collection. The term is traditional rather than geographically accurate. Some of the objects came from centres lying far beyond the confines of the Urals and Siberian regions. The area of their provenance embraced a vast territory, from the steppes roamed by early nomads of the Scythian circle in the 6th to the 4th centuries B.C. to the domains of medieval Iran and Byzantium.

Today we have no exact knowledge either of the original composition of Peter the Great's Siberian Collection, or even of the number of items in it: its history is still being studied. We know that it stayed in the *Kunstkammer*, where it grew continually until the fire of 1747 which destroyed the museum. The surviving items changed their whereabouts several times before 1859 when they found a permanent abode in the Hermitage. Here they got lost among the Museum's vast holdings, so that now a lot of painstaking research is needed to establish their identity as parts of Peter's collection, illustrating the early period of Russian collecting.

A set of fine blank weapons consisting of eight splendidly ornamented daggers wrought by armourers of different countries was kept in a special casket in Peter the Great's private collection. One of them, a 17th-centu-

Jean Marc Nattier (1685–1766).
Portrait of Peter the Great. 1717.
Oil on canvas. 142.5 × 110 cm.
The Hermitage

ry Indonesian *kris*, came from the Amsterdam collection of the apothecary Albert Seba. Another, of 16th-century Italian workmanship, was ascribed to no less a master than Benvenuto Cellini. A 16th-century carved ivory casket with scenes of The Fall contained a present to Peter from his ally, King Augustus II of Poland. It was a gold snuff-box with the portrait of Countess Cosel on the lid. Inside were two risqué pictures of the lady, "duae aliae figurae ex schola Aretini." The casket is now in the Hermitage; the snuff-box is missing, but an idea of the portrait can be formed from a drawing after it, preserved in the Russian Museum, St Petersburg. Another personal relic of Peter the Great, no longer extant, was a magnificent gold cup set with cameos and decorated with enamel — a gift of the Danish king, presented to the Tsar in 1716. In 1785, Catherine II, who had the cup from the *Kunstkammer*, caused its décor to be broken up and the gems, classified in accordance with the subjects, incorporated in her collection. Fortunately, however, we have at our disposal a watercolour of the 1730s by Ottmar Elliger. Recently the cup has been re-created on the basis of this drawing.

We have documentary evidence for some of Peter's acquisitions. It shows, for instance, that Rembrandt's masterpiece *David Parting from Jonathan* was purchased in Holland by Osip Solovyov, the Tsar's artistic agent. He bought it on 13 May 1716 at the Amsterdam sale of the collection of Jan van Beuningen, Director of the West India Company. The silver replica of Bernini's *La Fontana dei Quattro Fiume* was acquired by Savva Raguzinsky, Peter's diplomatic and commercial agent, and despatched to St Petersburg on board the frigate *Armont*. Raguzinsky also commissioned some sculptures from Venetian masters in 1717. In the spring of the same year, two statues by Giuseppe Torretto, *Diana* and *Narcissus*, arrived in the capital on board the frigate *John Judith* among a batch of one hundred sculptures bought for the decoration of Peter's Paradise — his Summer Gar-

dens. One of the Torretto statues has been preserved to our day; the other is known from a watercolour drawing commissioned by Savva Raguzinsky in Venice and later kept in Peter the Great's library. The famous *Venus* generally known as *Venus of Tauride*, unearthed in Rome in 1718, was acquired in the Eternal City. Unlike other sculptures, it was carried to Russia by land, in a special spring waggon ordered by the Tsar for its transportation.

In its earlier stage, Russian collectors exhibited a taste for what was then termed "curios". An example is provided by a miniature painting on copper recently identified as an item from the *Kunstkammer* collection. Fairly large for a miniature, it is a portrait of a lady, executed in 1661 by a Swedish artist who signed himself Qristoff Danielson. The portrait was accompanied by a set of 23 ovals in mica, painted with different details of costume and having an opening cut for the face of the model. When superimposed over the portrait on copper, each mica oval presented the sitter in a different apparel, all of them as extravagant as can be. The contemporary public easily recognized the model as Queen Christina of Sweden, the most famous woman of the 17th century.

Peter's example was followed by men of his entourage. Thus, Alexander Menshikov owned Alvise Tagliapetra's sculpture of *Justice*. From 1711 to 1725, his collection included a magnificent silver monstrance executed by the Revel master Hans Rissenberg in 1474. This work later entered the *Kunstkammer*, now it is in the Hermitage. James Bruce assembled a large collection of paintings, coins, various rarities, and archaeological objects. In the early years of the 18th century, he commissioned from the Nuremberg gem cutter Johann Dorsch a series of intaglio portraits on jasper, featuring a succession of Russian sovereigns from Prince Rurik to Tsar Ivan Alexeyevich. The series was carried on further in the 1730s by St Petersburg gem engravers, one of whom was Andrei Spiridonov. After Bruce's death, this collection joined the *Kunstkammer*, and then the Hermitage.

Lid of a snuff-box with the Portrait of Countess Cosel. 1730s. Drawing. The Russian Museum, St Petersburg. From the Kunstkammer collection

Catherine II's collecting activities may seem to represent a retrograde step when compared to Peter's. Whereas the Tsar had founded public museums, Catherine II kept her treasures in the imperial palace as a private collection accessible only to the elect. Peter had assembled all kinds of rare and artistic objects; Catherine's interests were confined to paintings, medals, and gems. The type of universal collection did not appeal to her. In the latter half of the 18th century, it was regarded as antiquated. Here is what Catherine said in criticism of her favourite Grigory Orlov's predilection for universal collecting: "I have often had to quarrel with him about his trying to cram all Nature into a cabinet, whereas even a palace would be too small for her!"

Comparison of the old and the new art collections as to size is a convincing argument in favour of the new approach to collecting. Peter's *Kunstkammer* contained approximately 250 paintings; Catherine's picture gallery, 2,080 in 1774; 2,658 in 1783; and 4,000 in 1796. The *Kunstkammer* collection of engraved gems numbered about a hundred items. By the end of Catherine's reign, she had 10,000 of her cherished "antiques" in her collection.

Apart from its purely artistic and educational aspects, the Russian Empress's collecting had some political connotations. Catherine felt highly gratified by the fact that the Gotzkowski collection, 225 canvases strong, proved to be beyond the reach of Frederick II, who had suffered a crushing defeat in the ruinous Seven Years' War. When Pierre Crozat's 500 paintings left Paris, the Empress gloried in the consciousness that Louis XV's minister could not afford this treasure; whereas she, although involved at the time in a war with Turkey, was able to thwart in this manner the French, Turkey's ally. Diderot wrote to Etienne Falconet, then in St Petersburg, fully aware that the content of his letter would be reported to Catherine: "I enjoy the most decided public hatred, and do you know why? It is that I send you pictures... Despite all the cries and all the peevish squalls I continue on my path...

The empress will acquire the Thiers collection in the midst of a costly war; see what will humiliate and confound them..."

While negotiating for the purchase in London of 300 antique sculptures of the Lyde Browne collection, the result of a lifetime's work, Catherine knew all about the debates in Parliament, demanding that the departure of the collection for Russia should be prevented. A desire to triumph over her rivals was by no means the least strong among the incentives for her collecting. A note of satisfied pride sounds in her letter to Melchior Grimm, dealing with her collection of engraved gems: "All the collections in Europe are but childishness when compared to ours!"

Some scholars go so far as to deny Catherine altogether any purely artistic interest or proper understanding of art's specific aims. Yet there are many facts showing that Catherine was not insensible to plastic beauty or the charm of colour in painting and that the simple joy known to all art collectors was not clouded for her by any political or educational superplans. One of the Empress's strong points was her skill in choosing associates. Catherine's immediate entourage included such art lovers as Dmitry Golitsyn, Ivan Shuvalov, Alexander Stroganov, and Nikolai Yusupov, all of them prominent collectors of their day.

Ivan Shuvalov, who rose to favour in the reign of Peter's daughter Elizabeth, formed his first art collection even before Catherine II's accession to the throne. Shuvalov's picture gallery was housed in his mansion on Italian Street. It was recorded in a canvas painted by Fiodor Rokotov around 1757 (copy of this painting is now in the History Museum, Moscow). Catherine II, at the time already an admirer of classical simplicity and architectural clarity, thought the Baroque decoration of Shuvalov's palace hopelessly outmoded and wrote with a dose of irony that "this house, large in itself, resembles in its ornamentation long sleeves of Alençon lace". The picture gal-

13

Narciso

F. dal Sig.r Giuseppe Torretti

Unknown artist. Narcissus. 1717.
India ink. 49 × 35 cm. The Academy
of Sciences Library, St Petersburg.
From the Peter the Great collection

lery was embellished with a painted plafond, mirrors, and gilded mouldings. Before the fireplace was a *trompe l'œil* picture by Pietro Rotari; it represented Shuvalov's Kalmyk servant holding his master's portrait. A formal portrait of Shuvalov from the brush of Jean Louis de Velly (now in the Russian Museum, St Petersburg) was at the window. The entire walls were covered with paintings, hung close to simulate an effect of tapestry decoration. On either side of the fireplace, in the upper row, were four pictures by Alessandro Magnasco, two of them from his *Bacchanalia* series (one is now in the Hermitage, and the other, in the Pushkin Museum of Fine Arts, Moscow); and the other two, from the series *The Halt of the Brigands* (now in the Hermitage). Identifiable at the bottom are the Hermitage canvases by Georg Rugendas; and in the middle row, Andrea Celesti's *Slaughter of the Innocents* (now in the Academy of Arts Museum, St Petersburg) and a remarkable work by the Flemish artist Michiel Sweerts, a canvas formerly known as *The Bankrupt*, and now defined as a self-portrait by the artist (now in the Hermitage).

After Catherine II's accession Shuvalov left Russia and until 1777 resided in Rome in a kind of honourable exile. Before his departure for Italy, he had his pictures transferred to the Academy of Arts, of which he was President. They came to the Hermitage much later, in the 1920s and '30s. In Rome, the Russian grandee plunged into the artistic life of that capital of the arts, making many friends among artists and collectors. He undertook to provide the Imperial Academy of Arts in St Petersburg with plaster casts of famous antique sculptures. Later on, the moulds he sent to the capital were used, by Catherine's command, in the casting of bronze statues to be seen even today at Tsarskoye Selo and Pavlovsk. Shuvalov also formed a collection of antique originals. On his return to Russia, they decorated his mansion on Italian Street. The traveller Johann Bernoulli, who visited Shuvalov in 1778, recorded in his notes some of the art works which

produced the strongest impression on him: a colossal head of Juno; a gigantic foot found near it; the helmeted head of a warrior, admired by Mengs who defined it as the head of Achilles; a Grecian altar; a piece from a mosaic floor; a mosaic imitating *The Doves* mentioned by Pliny; and lastly, painted ornamentation on pilasters, reproducing some of Raphael's arabesques in the Vatican. All these antiquities are now in the Hermitage. In 1785, they were bought by the Empress and transferred from Shuvalov's palace to Tsarskoye Selo.

Particularly noteworthy is Bernoulli's mention of "Raphael's arabesques". These were copies of some of the decorations of the celebrated Loggie in the Vatican, which were later reproduced in full in St Petersburg, at the desire of the Empress. Giovanni-Battista Piranesi, the theorist of Neo-classicism, dedicated his set of engravings to "A Sua Eccelenza il Sig. General Schouvaloff Promotor delle Belle Arti..." At the request of Catherine II, the Ober-Kammerherr sent her from Rome twelve volumes of Piranesi's engravings, entitled *Vasi, candelabri, cippi, sarcophagi, tripodi, lucerne ed ornamenti antichi, disegnati ed incisi dal Cav. G.-B. Piranesi, publicati l'anno MDCCLXXVIII*. Referring to her new interest Catherine wrote to her Paris correspondent Melchior Grimm: "Now Piranesi is most *à la mode*. 'Tis a pity there are but fifteen volumes of his work." In view of all this, it would be difficult to deny Shuvalov's influence upon the Empress's artistic interests, even upon the formation of her personal taste.

Nor could she escape the influence on the part of Count Alexander Stroganov, afterwards President of the Academy of Arts. His palace on the Moika river was, on the evidence of contemporary observers, the favourite resort of men of good taste. Artists used to converge there, including such celebrities as Alexander Varnek, Vasily Shebuyev, Alexei Egorov, Dmitry Levitsky, Stepan Shchukin, Jean Mosnier, Joseph Vien, and Jean-Baptiste Thomas de Thomon.

Giuseppe Torretto (1664–1743).
Diana. Marble. Height 60 cm;
length 109 cm. The Hermitage.
From the Peter the Great collection

Count Stroganov travelled abroad extensively, making acquisitions for his gallery both at various sales and directly from painters at their studios. He commissioned a sculptural portrait of the Empress from Jean Houdon, and another from Jean Tassaert, to whom he recommended that a figure intended to be Minerva, patroness of the arts, be turned into Catherine II. This ruse, revealing in the young art lover a crafty courtier, was by no means exceptional. Thus, while negotiating for the purchase of Francesco Solimena's *Allegory of the Glorious Reign* (now in the Hermitage), he desired that a change be made in the central medallion with the sovereign's portrait. Originally the portrait represented Louis XIV, Le Roi soleil. In the Catalogue of his collection, Stroganov made the following entry: "This picture had belonged to Mr Bouret, who, for love for Louis XV, had the portrait of this Prince put in place of that of Charles V (*sic*). For my part, I have had the head of Louis XV erased in order to put there that of the Empress Catherine II."

The Hermitage owns a watercolour picture of the Stroganov gallery, made in 1793 by Andrei Voronikhin, responsible for rebuilding it. In 1793, the owner of the gallery published a printed catalogue of his collection, one of the earliest works of the kind to appear in Russia. In Europe, descriptions of private collections were generally compiled after the owner's death, by way of preparation for a sale. Meanwhile, Catherine II's collection of paintings was being catalogued at the Hermitage. Regrettably, the complete text compiled by Count Ernest Münnich (1773–83) and Franz Labensky (1797) remained in manuscript. It is preserved in the Museum's Record Office. In 1800, Stroganov published a new edition of his catalogue, with 115 canvases recorded against the original 87.

Stroganov was an ardent admirer of Neo-classicism, and this determined his choice of pictures. Paintings of the "lower orders", like genre scenes or still lives, were practically excluded from his gallery. The collection closed with French 17th-century works, containing neither Watteaus, nor Chardins, nor Bouchers. Exceptions were made for 18th-century landscapists, such as Joseph Vernet or Hubert Robert. Nicolas Poussin's *Flight into Egypt* (now in the Hermitage) was the pride of the collection, a model of what its owner regarded as the ideal in painting. He wrote: "This wise, noble and vast composition of the pictures which I am describing here clearly asserts the equality of Poussin's genius to that of Raphael. An erudite artist who ever drew from ancient monuments the style and grandeur which lie therein..."

In the 1770s, the Stroganov collection was enriched by a rare example of antique art, a marble sarcophagus decorated with scenes of the myth of Achilles. It had been discovered in Chios during the Russo-Turkish War and was believed to be the coffin of Homer. Andrei Voronikhin placed it at the top of a hill in the park of Stroganov's villa on the Greater Neva, where the sarcophagus presented a most effective picture. Stroganov's palace on the Moika contained not only his famous picture gallery, but also a number of rich numismatic, archaeological, and mineralogical collections arranged in a special set of rooms.

Prince Nikolai Yusupov was among Catherine's closest associates. He travelled a lot and in 1783 was appointed the Empress's diplomatic agent at Turin, Venice, and Naples. Yusupov cleverly combined his diplomatic duties with the activities of an art collector and patron of the arts. In Rome he established contacts with such artists as Pompeo Batoni, Domenico Corvi, Anton Maron, Gavin Hamilton, Angelica Kauffmann, and the sculptor Antonio Canova. Similar contacts linked Yusupov with the art world of Paris: Jean-Baptist Greuze, Jean Fragonard, Elizabeth Vigée Lebrun, Charles Guérin, Jacques Louis David. His travels brought Yusupov in contact with philosophers and poets, and thus with the dominant ideas of the age. Beaumarchais dedicated to him *L'Epître* (1776). Yusupov visited Voltaire at Ferney, produced a good impression, and returned full of admiration for the old

philosopher and all that he said. Catherine wrote to Voltaire: "I must first tell You that if You are content with Prince Yusupov, I must say of him that he is enchanted with the good welcome which You gave him, and with all You said during the time he had the pleasure of seeing You." Some passages in the Empress's correspondence with her diplomat sound like confidences freely exchanged between two friends who see entirely eye-to-eye. "My lord Prince Yusupov, I have received your letter in due time. I have waited for a suitable occasion to send you an answer. Well, Pichler, Weder, and Amastini are engaged in increasing my small collection, which has been enlarged this autumn by the purchase of the Cabinet of the Duke of Orleans. With three finger rings you sent me for my name-day, my small collection numbers 7,817 gems... Men of learning and ignoramuses alike are turning antiquaries, and it is amusing to watch them rummage through heaps of books, sometimes only to dig up the merest trifles. But all this is nothing compared to what I have to say further. General Mamonov himself took up stone cutting, and by way of experiment engraved, to Leberecht's greatest amazement, a lovely intaglio; now he is labouring at a cameo with the head of Minerva, which has not yet been completed."

Yusupov's palace on the Fontanka, built by Giacomo Quarenghi, was described in detail by the German traveller Georg Reimers, who visited it in 1800. The art treasures housed there at the time of his visit were transferred in the 19th century to Yusupov's mansion on the Moika and the family estate at Arkhangelskoye near Moscow; after 1925 some pieces entered the Hermitage, others the Russian Museum, St Petersburg, and the Pushkin Museum of Fine Arts, Moscow. In the palace on the Fontanka, an entire room was hung with twelve large canvases — full-scale preliminary versions for Hackaert's *Chesme* series painted for the memorial Chesme Room in the Great Palace at Peterhof. A special hall was given over to canvases by the old masters, Pieter Paul Rubens, An-

thonis van Dyck (now at Arkhangelskoye), Claude Lorrain (now in the Pushkin Museum of Fine Arts, Moscow). Arranged apart from the rest were Alexeyev's landscapes in the manner of Canaletto (now some are at Arkhangelskoye, others in the Russian Museum, St Petersburg). Giovanni Tiepolo's plafonds and paintings illustrating the story of Cleopatra (now at Arkhangelskoye) occupied a separate room. Yusupov's gallery of works by contemporary masters included Heinrich Füger's *Portrait of the Collector* (now in the Hermitage) and three canvases by Louis Boilly (one, *A Game of Billiards*, is now in the Hermitage).

Like Count Stroganov, Prince Yusupov was one of the leading arbiters in questions of art of his day. In 1789, Catherine II appointed him Director of her Tapestry Works; in 1792, she made him Director of the Glass and Porcelain Factories; and in 1797, Director of the Imperial Hermitage.

It was small wonder that the members of old aristocratic families, while building costly mansions for themselves, should fill them with treasures of art: in this they followed family tradition. Prince Alexander Bezborodko had no aristocratic ancestors. By contrast, he was himself fortunate enough in his career to lay the basis of the rise to greatness of such houses as those of the Bezborodkos, Kochubeis, Kushelev-Bezborodkos, and Miloradoviches. And yet it could not be denied that the newly fledged "aristocrat from Malorossia (i.e., the Ukraine)" was one of the most prominent art collectors and patrons of art in 18th-century Russia. He commissioned their most brilliant works from such portraitists as Dmitry Levitsky, Vasily Borovikovsky, Fedot Shubin, Jacques Dominique Rochette, and Johann-Baptist Lampi. He was the third owner of Etienne Falconet's *Cupid* (now in the Hermitage) after Catherine II and Count Stroganov. This sculpture is the author's own version; one of its former owners was Marchioness de Pompadour. The pedestal is inscribed with two lines by Voltaire:

Qui que tu sois, voici ton maître,
Il l'est, le fut ou doit l'être.

The poet Gavrila Derzhavin dedicated several Anacreontic lyrics to the statue. One of them is called *Croesus' Cupid* and runs somewhat like this:

I at Croesus' saw young Eros:
His poor face awash with tears.
Midst the marble grotto
Hails of arrows raining round...

Is his flame then without power?
Vain his stream of dang'rous tears?
Woe! He must own he is beaten:
Croesus has no love to give.

A letter to Semion Vorontsov is a kind of summing-up of Bezborodko's activity as collector. "By dint of hot zeal, my friends' aid, and approximately one hundred thousand spent in the course of less than three years, I have formed a good collection, surpassing that of Stroganov's both in number and in quality..."

The traveller Reimers, whose work has been already referred to, left us a description of the art works assembled in Bezborodko's house (now the Museum of Communications): "The Bezborodko Mansion is wondrous in its expensive furniture, which decorated... the Trianon... the Palais Royale... the works of Charles Boule... bronze statues by Houdon, the Sèrves vase of blue porcelain decorated with bronze and white bisquit which is so notable for its great height... the marble bust of the prince, the work of Shubin... 16 canvases by Vernet, largely marine subjects... a marble Cupid, slyly lifting its finger to its mouth... Jordaens' *Bean King,* Dou's *Dutch Woman by a Door...* "

After Alexander Bezborodko's death, his collection was split among the houses of the Kochubeis, Miloradov-iches, Moussine-Poushkins, Lobanov-Rostovskys, Paske-viches, despite his express desire that his heirs keep it intact. Some of them eventually found their way to the Hermitage. In 1922 a group of works once owned by Nikolai Kushelev-Bezborodko were transferred from the Academy of Arts; they included *The Bean King* by Jacob Jordaens, *The Adoration of the Infant Christ* by Pieter Brueghel, and *Christ Crowned with Thorns* by Rubens. A huge vase of Sèvres porcelain, the pride of the original owner, entered the Museum in 1915 from the collection of Irene Paskevich along with *The Spoiled Child* by Jean-Baptiste Greuze. Some of the items of the Bezborodko collection are now far beyond the confines of Russia: in Philadelphia (Gerard Terborch, *A Woman and a Soldier*), in Paris (Joseph Vernet, *Marine*), in Prague (George Dawe, *Young Woman on a Balcony*). Bezborodko's aesthetic credo was formulated by him in a letter to Alexander Vorontsov, expressing a hope that his activity "may show to posterity that we of this present age and of this our land were men of taste".

It is not to be wondered at that Catherine's closest associates were true connoisseurs of the fine arts: they modelled their tastes on those of the Empress. In a letter of 1786, Catherine owned to Grimm: "In my old age I shall become an antiquarian in the full sense of the term." However, her efforts were not always rewarded with success: occasionally things went wrong. Thus, in 1773 the Empress commissioned from the French artist Charles Clérisseau (through the agency of Etienne Falconet and Nicolas Cochin) a set of drawings for a house in the antique style, decorated on the outside exactly like the mansion of a Roman, with the interiors furnished as nearly as possible after the antique. She expressly wished that the building, which was to be a "pavilion in the garden, should be not too large, nor too small".

On receiving the Empress's clearly expressed instructions, Clérisseau sent back an enormous series of drawings for a huge Roman palace, filling eighteen large cases,

Portrait of Mikhail Vorontsov.
Lomonosov's workshop. Mosaics.
59 × 50 cm. The Hermitage

and charged a correspondingly high fee for his work. Catherine thought that she had been misunderstood. Falconet wrote to the Ambassador Dmitry Golitsyn that the order was only for a garden pavilion. When the conflict reached a stage where it might attract the attention of journalists, it was with great difficulty hushed up through the mediation of influential persons and diplomats. The Empress had to pay Clérisseau's inordinate fee. Five years later she wrote to Grimm, seemingly forgetful of the quarrel: "I shall be very curious to see from him something other than the plan of a house of a Roman emperor... and if his portfolios were for sale I would with pleasure make their purchase... Loosen Clérisseau's tongue, that he should say what in his portfolio best pleased Joseph the Second." Thus, the artist was forgiven, and the first works he sent pleased the Empress. In 1780, she wrote to Paris: " Very well, send us some Clérisseaus, for 'tis a delicious dish." Catherine II had made Clérisseau Honorary Associate of the St Petersburg Academy of Arts and conferred upon him the title of First Architect to the Court. Over a thousand drawings by the artist were housed in the Hermitage; seventeen gouaches of monuments of ancient Rome decorated the Empress's boudoir in the Winter Palace. However, in 1785 a new row flared up over Clérisseau's fee. This time the artist sought the protection of the Prince of Anhalt-Dessau, a relative of Catherine's. Here is what she wrote to Grimm concerning this matter: "I found these two letters, to tell you true, a little singular; I had thought that Seigneur Clérisseau would be content with my dealings, for the sale was good and honest; that surplus which he sent me, I recall not if I requested this, ordered it, or agreed to his suggestion... That which I owe Clérisseau you should pay him and ask him to send me of his work only when I request it of him, for else he could leave on my hands many more high-flown things with the same pretensions, and I am not always in the humour to reply to those who interfere in my affairs without my asking

them." The Empress, only recently full of admiration for Clérisseau's work, now wrote to Grimm: "I wish to have no more of his works, and he should send me no more... I beg you to flee this man like the plague!"

A somewhat similar episode took place when the Roman antiquary Thomas Jenkins offered to sell the Empress a collection of Correggios. The very fact that the offer was not for a single canvas but for a whole batch of them ought to have set Catherine on her guard. Yet she instructed her agent Johann Reiffenstein to examine the collection, together with the experts Mengs, Maron, Batoni, and Hackaert. When the pictures arrived in St Petersburg and proved not to be authentic, Catherine's indignation knew no bounds. In her anger, she wrote to Grimm: "I had wished to say that the pictures sent here are not rubbish, but this has been established... Living in the middle of Rome and its artists and seeing every day of the year masterpieces by great men, Reiffenstein understands no more about pictures than a newborn infant, while we who are forced to stride up and down the galleries of the Hermitage can tell good from bad at a quick glance." She laid a strict injunction upon Reiffenstein and Grimm alike to have nothing to do with Mr Jenkins. After that, when Reiffenstein offered the Empress to buy a colossal statue, *Jupiter Enthroned*, she — cautious after the tricks played on her by Roman antiquaries — rejected the offer. However, such is the irony of fate that in the reign of her great-grandson Alexander II the sculpture was nevertheless acquired for the Hermitage.

As we have seen, Catherine could be quite merciless where her collecting interests were concerned. In 1779, an opportunity occurred to buy a canvas by Mengs under questionable circumstances. The work, representing Perseus and Andromeda, had been painted on commission for a rich Englishman, Sir William Watkin. It was displayed for public inspection at Mengs's studio in Rome and was a great success. Afterwards the painting was

Andrei Voronikhin (1760–1814).
Picture Gallery in Alexander
Stroganov's Palace. Watercolour.
43.3 × 56.2 cm. The Hermitage

carried to Livorno and placed on board a ship bound for England. Near the French coast the ship was seized by pirates. Their loot was confiscated by the French government. At this point Baron Grimm, Catherine's Parisian agent, made his appearance on the stage. He approached the French minister of foreign affairs with the proposition that the canvas be sold to the Empress of Russia. Catherine's letter to him betrays a certain sense of discomfort. She wrote: "I find that you and M. de Vergennes are ready, to please me, to rob an honest English gentleman; decidedly I am much obliged to you for the pleasure which you have planned for me in this case and in many others... but my conscience strikes me a little that it will be done at the cost to a fellow man. If the good Englishman appeals to me, I shall give him his picture." It does not seem that Sir William Watkin took courage to address himself to the Empress, for his picture adorns the Hermitage collection to this day.

We do not know when and how the idea of creating a picture gallery at the Hermitage first occurred to Catherine. However, there can be little doubt that it was suggested by the policy and practice of Peter the Great: his interest in collecting, the foundation of the *Kunstkammer* museum and the Picture House at Oranienbaum, where she resided as Grand Princess. The fact that the creation of the Hermitage picture gallery began when Catherine's reign was but a year old, speaks for itself. The gallery was obviously regarded as an important link in a series of measures intended to demonstrate to the world that Russia had every right to be described as a European country, a right Catherine claimed in the first lines of her *Nakaz* (Instruction en vue de l'elaboration d'un Code de lois). Other steps taken by Catherine with the same purpose included the setting up of a law-making commission, the invitation of the philosopher D'Alembert to the post of tutor to the heir (which he was wise enough to decline) and a proposal to print the *Encyclopédie, ou Dictionarie raisonné des sciences, des arts et de métiers,* con-

demned by the Parliament of Paris. The results of this policy were not long to manifest themselves. The Encyclopedists, who voiced the public opinion of Europe, were loud in their praises of Catherine's enlightened rule. Diderot even wrote in a letter to Voltaire, that, in contrast to France, where philosophy was persecuted, in "Scythia" it was patronized.

We have already noted the fairly common view of Catherine's collecting, accentuating its pragmatic aspect and wholly denying her all power of artistic discrimination. There are statements by contemporaries and Catherine's own declarations to this effect, insisting that the Empress, in the words of the Prince de Ligne, "has no knowledge in either painting or music". While recording these statements, the Prince de Ligne, more keen-sighted than the others, suggested that here we are dealing with a pose deliberately adopted by Catherine so as to ensure for herself a complete freedom of judgement: "The Empress made use of this pretension to ignorance in order to mock the doctors, academies, the ill-educated and false experts."

We have already dwelt at some length on the problem of the influence exerted over Catherine II by Ivan Shuvalov, a statesman of the previous reign. Yet for all his undeniable influence, the Empress's attitude towards him was clearly not uncritical, especially in matters of taste and artistic judgement. In 1758, Catherine, then Grand Princess, had referred to "la maison du chambellan Jean Chouvaloff" in the following words: "the house of Chamberlain Jean Shuvalov... just recently finished and in which the master used all his taste to the full despite which the house was without taste and indeed quite bad, albeit very richly contrived. There were many pictures, but the greater part were copies. Externally, this house in itself resembled long sleeves of Alençon lace, it was so covered with ornamentation."

But after her blunder with the purchase of a whole collection of pseudo-Correggios, Catherine was obvious-

19

Sarcophagus ("Coffin of Homer").
2nd century. Marble. 243 × 168 cm.
The Hermitage. From the Alexander
Stroganov collection

ly nervous about Shuvalov's reaction: "The pictures are such rubbish," she wrote to Grimm, "that Martinelli and I found nothing more pressing than to send the worst of them to the furniture store before the arrival of those malicious wags of which there are a good number even around us." Echoes of furious clashes of opinion between Catherine and Shuvalov resound in another letter to Grimm: "This great Chamberlain puts around rumours that the priest [Reiffenstein] is buying too dear, for he, the gr. ch., has never bought but rubbish, and that very cheap; and this rubbish he has wished to pass off to us as good works. It is surprising moreover that, having passed so many years in Rome, he is so little formed as to taste and understanding." A person lacking in taste and understanding cultivated by years of exercise could hardly have dared to enter into argument in this decided manner with a connoisseur of recognized authority.

In the building up of the Hermitage collection, Catherine enrolled the services of enlightened diplomats, in addition to her vast network of artistic agents like Grimm, Diderot, François Tronchin, and Reiffenstein. The most active among the former was Prince Dmitry Golitsyn (1734–1803). He had resided in Paris since his youth and in 1763 was made Russian plenipotentiary in France. It was he who made a contract with Etienne Falconet regarding a monument to Peter the Great (1766); he commissioned from Jean Chardin the *Still-life with Attributes of the Arts* (1765); and he bought from Greuze his *Paralytic*, highly praised by Diderot. But his greatest achievement was the acquisition of Rembrandt's monumental canvas *The Return of the Prodigal Son.*

What most amazed European connoisseurs, diplomats, monarchs, and the general public in Catherine II was her habit of buying whole collections of art works, the priceless heritage of Europe. These triumphs got Russia talked about no less than the triumphs of Russian arms at Chesme and Kagul. Of these collections, only one, purchased from the Berlin merchant Johann Ernest

Gotzkowski, was formed within a relatively short time (1755–64), expressly for Frederick II; whereas the others, like the carefully planned collections of Carl Cobentzl and Prince Charles de Ligne, acquired in 1768 at Brussels, and that of Count Heinrich Brühl, bought in 1769 at Dresden, had been built up over several generations. The same is true of the collection of François Tronchin of Geneva, purchased with the aid of Golitsyn and Diderot in 1770.

A year later, Dmitry Golitsyn, by then Russian Ambassador to the Hague, prepared a new "peaceful triumph" for Catherine II: he bought the best canvases from the collection of Gerrit Braamkamp, put up for sale at Amsterdam. The pictures were shipped to St Petersburg, and the Empress looked forward to their arrival, when the ship was wrecked and sank in the waters of the Baltic. Golitsyn wrote to François Tronchin how he had hoped that the information of the loss of the entire collection might be erroneous: it was rumoured in St Petersburg that the Empress sent her representatives to the spot and that they were in time to salvage all the paintings. Unfortunately, Golitsyn was misinformed — perhaps not unintentionally — by his St Petersburg correspondents. In December 1771, he wrote to Tronchin another letter, with a different account of the matter. By that time he had learned from a reliable source that the ship sank a few hours after running aground, and that not a single painting had been saved. Curiously enough, the cause of the calamity was the inordinate piety of the captain. He navigated his ship without proper local knowledge, using a sounding-lead. But when the hour of prayers came, he left the navigation to the care of a sailor or even a ship-boy and went down to join the rest of the crew at their devotions. They were in the midst of these devotions when the ship struck a stone bank and was wrecked.

Judging by her European correspondence, Catherine II, whose main concern was with the impression produced in Europe by her loss of Le Temple des Arts, as Bra-

*Ares. Roman copy of
a 5th-century B.C. original. Marble.
Height 92 cm. The Hermitage.
From the Ivan Shuvalov collection*

amkamp's collection was pompously designated, took things in a more resigned spirit. She wrote to Voltaire that the loss amounted to no more than 60,000 roubles and that it was not the only loss she had had to sustain in the acquisition of art works. The only way, she felt, would be to accept what could not be helped, and be comforted, and seek for consolation elsewhere. And the consolation was not long in coming. In 1770, Antoine Crozat, Baron de Thiers, died in Paris. He was the owner of a magnificent picture gallery, founded in the late 18th century by the banker Pierre Crozat (1665–1740), who freely lavished his money on the most expensive art treasures. Tronchin advised Golitsyn and Grimm to buy the entire Crozat collection before the sale was declared. Diderot was to effect the transaction. After a year and a half spent in negotiations, a deal was struck. The entire collection was bought for 460,000 livres. In June 1772, the paintings arrived in St Petersburg aboard the *Swallow*. In the same year, a sensational sale was held in Paris of the collection of the once all-powerful French minister, the Duc de Choiseul. Diderot wrote to his friend Falconet, describing the situation, that the removal of Baron de Thiers' collection to St Petersburg, along with the rivalry of M. de Laborde and Mme Du Barry, as well as other circumstances connected with the personality of M. de Choiseul, resulted in an incredible rise in prices at the sale. About 50 canvases were bought for the sum of 440,000 livres; whereas three months before, 500 had been bought for 460,000 livres. No wonder, he remarked, that the legatees of Baron de Thiers were in a flying rage.

Catherine II, well satisfied with the acquisition of the Crozat collection, could not forgo the pleasure of triumphing over Russia's main political enemy. Diderot bought for her eleven canvases at the Choiseul sale, placing the Hermitage gallery on a par with the richest European collections. The treasures assembled by European art collectors over centuries became the property of Russia by dint of a single superior stroke of strategy, uniting the expert knowledge, liberality, and daring of the Empress with her agents' purposefulness and business acumen. Her reply to a letter from Voltaire shows that Catherine was perfectly aware both of the effect her policy produced on Europe and also of its importance for the prestige of Russia. Voltaire had wondered if it were wise to buy such large numbers of pictures. Catherine admitted that at the moment it might indeed be better to limit her purchases. But she was afraid to miss her opportunities, which might never occur again. Besides, she argued, she kept her private purse strictly separate from the state treasury; and with things properly managed, a great country was always able to afford all kinds of expenses. It was owing to this attitude on the part of the Empress that the Hermitage picture gallery was fortunate enough to receive a number of paintings once incorporated in some of the leading collections dating from the Italian Renaissance and Baroque periods: *Portrait of an Actor* by Domenico Fetti from the Gonzaga collection in Mantua; *Birth of St John the Baptist* by Tintoretto from that of Cardinal Mazarin in Paris; *Youth of the Madonna* by Guido Reni; *Judith* by Giorgione; *The Lamentation* by Paolo Veronese, and *St George* by Raphael, formerly owned by King Charles I of England. The Empress undertook a series of fundamental alterations in her Winter Palace, so as to make room for her rapidly increasing collections. Catherine II's hermitage had long outgrown the limits of a secluded pavilion for supper parties among an intimate circle of friends, as well as those of a private cabinet of an enlightened connoisseur. It was gradually developing in the direction of its present status: a grandiose art museum.

In the beginning Catherine used to dwell on the strict privacy and secluded atmosphere of her hermitage, located above the first floor of the Winter Palace. Thus, she wrote in a letter to Grimm: "I have a labyrinth of apartments although I am but one; there is in all this an inveterate luxury... it has been baptized the Imperial Museum,

Johann-Baptist Lampi I (1751–1830). Portrait of Catherine II. 1793. Oil on canvas. 290 × 208 cm. The Hermitage

and when you are here there is so much to see that you cannot leave... there the mice and I can look at it all." That was in 1777, and here is what the Empress wrote to the same person thirteen years later: "My museum in the Hermitage consists, without the pictures and Raphael Loggias, of 38,000 books, 10,000 carved gems and 10,000 drawings."

The name "Hermitage" was first applied to the pavilion facing the Neva, part of the building constructed by Jean-Baptiste Vallin de la Mothe between 1763 and 1767 and now known as the Small Hermitage. Two galleries flanking the Hanging Garden — a roof garden resting on the vaults of the lower storey — contained the Empress's collection of paintings. In the 1770s and '80s, the picture gallery was gradually transferred to a suite in the new building by Velten, the Old Hermitage, stretched along the Neva. Between 1783 and 1787, the Hermitage Theatre was built on the opposite bank of the Winter Canal; it was connected to the Old Hermitage by a gallery resting upon arches, stretching across the canal. On the days of theatrical performances at court, the picture rooms functioned as drawing-rooms and foyer. The Hermitage collections became increasingly involved with the pageantry of court life; nothing was left of their former privacy and seclusion. The discrepancy between the grand scale of her magnificent museum and the name "Hermitage" was observed in Catherine's lifetime. In his reminiscences the French Ambassador, Count Sègur, depicted in glowing colours the contrast between the notion of a hermit's humble abode and the luxury of Catherine's palace, with its spacious halls and galleries, its magnificent furnishings, its abundance of paintings by great artists, and its charming indoor garden where the verdure, the flowers, and the birds' songs seemed to be harbingers of Italian spring amidst the snows of the North. He did not fail to note the well-stocked library whose contents showed that "the Hermit of these parts" preferred the light of philosophy to monastic exercises;

or the beautiful theatre hall which seemed to be a smaller version of antique amphitheatre at Vicenza.

It may be safely averred that no other part of Catherine's museum was so well documented as her gem collection. Her passion for the "antiques", as they were called in her day, was constant and enduring. The Empress jokingly referred to it as "gourmandise", "maladie", and to her glyptic collection as a "gouffre" (abyss). In the spring of 1782, she wrote to Grimm: "My little collection of engraved stones is such that yesterday four people with difficulty carried two baskets filled with drawers containing around half of the collection; and that you should be in no doubt, you should know that these baskets are those in which they carry wood to the rooms here in winter and that the drawers overflowed the baskets; from this you can judge the gluttonous greediness which has taken hold of us in this sphere... we have them [engraved stones] of a size of over two *vershoks*." This passage, characterizing the scale of Catherine's collecting, is also illustrative of the next phase in the building up of the Museum, when the collections were in the act of transportation to the Velten building, the Old Hermitage of today.

Special museum cabinets for gems and medals, richly ornamented with gilt bronze mounts, were commissioned from the German furniture maker David Roentgen. Catherine wrote: "Not a day goes by on which I do not wander around my cupboards; one must gain from them so much knowledge, to which there is no end." The Empress's greatest success came in 1787, when she bought the glyptic collection of the Duke of Orleans. A family collection, one of the most famous in Europe, it had been enriched in 1741 by the purchase of the cabinet of engraved gems once owned by Pierre Crozat. In this way Crozat's gems came to join his paintings in the Hermitage. Count Evgraf Komarovsky was perfectly justified in calling the newly acquired gem collection numbering 1,500 items, "one of the most notable possessions of the Hermitage". Catherine II started the work

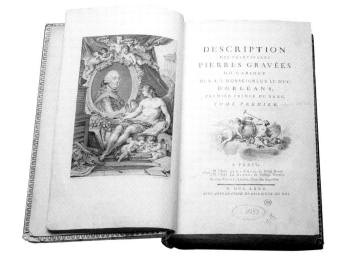

of systematic arrangement and study of the Hermitage collections and made it a part of her daily occupations. In a letter to Grimm, she said: "God alone knows what pleasure there is in handling all that every day; it hides endless knowledge." This activity was not interrupted even in summer, when the Court moved to Tsarskoye Selo. The "antiques", along with the most necessary books, followed the Empress in a special carriage.

In 1795, Catherine already had at her disposal a manuscript catalogue of her glyptic collection. It was compiled (in French) by her librarian Alexander Luzhkov. She proudly informed Grimm that "all this is arranged systematically beginning with the Egyptians and passing through all the mythologies, fabulous and non-fabulous histories up to the present day... perhaps the taking of Prague will have its place there in time, as well as such heroes as Suvorov, Fersen and Derfelden; Valeriyan [Zubov] is already there".

At the Empress's command, Luzhkov was "accepted" as a member to the Academy of Sciences "for his thorough study of the antiques".

The gems of Catherine's collection were reproduced in glass paste by Georg König, artist and chemist, and the gem cutter Karl Leberecht, working in the Empress's private suite. Tens of thousands of similar reproductions, forming counterparts of all the European glyptic cabinets, were ordered from London. König and Dietrich Zöllner made a portrait of Grigory Potiomkin and Catherine wrote to her favourite, then in the Crimea: "I am sending you a portrait, engraved after a gem, of the conqueror of Ochakov; both the gem and the portrait have been cut in my Hermitage." Some persons of Catherine's immediate entourage took up gem cutting and succeeded in mastering its difficult techniques, and in another letter she tells Potiomkin of the emergence of a new gem cutter, a young favourite who replaced him in his absence: "This is to certify that I have witnessed (otherwise I would never have believed it) Alexander Dmitriyev-

Mamonov cut with his own hands the carnelian seal sent with the present testimonial; and that Leberecht had no part whatever in this work." Catherine's daughter-in-law, Maria Fiodorovna, showed no mean ability as a gem engraver. She executed portraits of her husband, Crown Prince Paul (afterwards Paul I), their sons Alexander and Constantine, and Catherine herself as Minerva. The last-mentioned work won the Empress's approval: "the cameo is a very good likeness and excellently cut," she wrote.

Nor could Catherine's favourites help sharing her passion for collecting, some of them forming major private galleries. The name of Potiomkin, for instance, is associated with the formation of the Hermitage collection of fine and applied English art. His acquisitions included a huge wine-cooler by Philip Rollos, the Peacock Clock by James Cox, prints by James Walker, and paintings by artists of the English School. The first of the canvases came in 1779 with the Robert Walpole collection (from his ancestral seat at Houghton Hall), sold to the Empress by the grandson of the once all-powerful English minister. The Hermitage picture gallery had by that time reached a stage where the unavoidable lacunae — notably in English 18th-century painting—required filling. In 1785, the English diplomat Lord Carysfort, acting on behalf of the Empress, offered a commission to Sir Joshua Reynolds. In his letter to the painter he wrote: "I have expressed my regret at every visit to the Hermitage that the gallery should not have a single example of the work of the painters of the English School. I am proud to say that I turned Her Majesty's attention to our painters." As a result of these negotiations, Reynolds painted for Catherine *The Infant Hercules Killing Snakes*, an allegory of the fast-growing Russian might, and for Potiomkin *The Continence of Scipio*. The London artist, in fixing his choice on the didactic subject of Virtue in a Sovereign for the latter picture, was possibly guided by the knowledge that Potiomkin's gallery already included a painting on the

Title page: Description des pierres gravées par Alfonso Miliotty antiquary. St. Pétersbourg. Late 18th century. Engraving. The Hermitage

theme, Pierre Mignard's *The Magnanimity of Alexander the Great*, acquired from the Duchess of Kingston (now in the Hermitage). In August 1789, both canvases by Reynolds arrived in St Petersburg on board the frigate *Friendship*. Later, Potiomkin's collection came to comprise one more painting by Reynolds, his lovely *Cupid Untying the Zone of Venus* (now in the Hermitage). After the favourite's death in 1792, these canvases entered the Hermitage picture gallery. Other paintings from Potiomkin's collection which came to the Hermitage included a portrait of Piotr Potiomkin by Godfrey Kneller, *Landscape with Aeneas and Dido* by Thomas Jones, and *Seashore* by William Marlowe, all acquired by the former owner at different times.

In 1780, the English painter Richard Brompton came to Russia at the invitation of Catherine II. He made a portrait of the Empress (now in the Hermitage) and one of Countess Aleksandra Branicka, Potiomkin's niece (now in the Vorontsov Palace, Alupka). For her Chesme Palace Catherine commissioned from him a programme picture of her grandsons Alexander and Constantine. Executed in the interval between the two wars with Turkey, the painting was intended to proclaim that Russia was firmly set on her chosen course. Catherine wrote to Grimm, with great satisfaction: "Brompton, the English painter, is established here and has great talent; he is a student of Mengs; he has painted my two grandsons and it is a charming picture; the eldest amuses himself with cutting the Gordian knot, and the other has impudently placed on his shoulder Constantine's colours; this picture looks no worse in my gallery beside the Van Dycks." To prove her point, the Empress commissioned from Brompton a replica of the programme canvas for Grimm. Her correspondent was eloquent in his expressions of gratitude for the gift: "Everyone finds this picture charming," he wrote back, "and come to me in crowds to see it." It was not only the purely artistic effect that gave so much satisfaction in St Petersburg, but also the transparent political message effectively conveyed by the picture,

charged with a threatening spirit against Turkey and her ally in the war, France. As the author of the *Ode on the Taking of Izmail* saw it, the Empress set herself the aim.

To restore Athena to Athens,
And Constantine, to Constantine's city!

During the period between 1786 and 1796, Catherine enriched her glyptic collection by nearly two hundred gems wrought by contemporary artists, the Englishmen William and Charles Brown. Particularly valuable for us are their works featuring Russian subjects, e.g. equestrian statue of Peter the Great by Falconet, several portraits of Catherine II, an allegory of Potiomkin's victories in Russo-Turkish wars, and another on the favourite's death.

Outstanding in the history of Russian collecting was the activity of Alexander Lanskoi, the Empress's youthful favourite. His period of favour lasted for about six years, the whole of which time was marked by passionate collecting. A facetious passage in one of Grimm's letters to Catherine refers to Lanskoi's enthusiasm: "As for his illnesses, the result of a general gluttony, I have seen most reliable symptoms in my quality as chief imperial doctor in these sorts of infirmities." At first, as a timid novice, Lanskoi only dared to assemble prints, but before long he acquired a strong taste for general collecting. We know that prior to commissioning from Greuze a miniature after Vigilius Erichsen's equestrian portrait of the Empress, Lanskoi had a copy of the canvas made by Dmitry Levitsky and sent it to Grimm in Paris. The latter gave Catherine a jocular warning of her favourite's "malady" growing upon him: "And thus illnesses become incurable." Lanskoi's appetites were not satisfied by his collection of miniature reproductions of the best Hermitage paintings. In 1781, he came to own a whole picture gallery, bought for him in Paris from Count Baudouin and containing 119 canvases, nine Rembrandts and six Van Dycks included. Regrettably, some of these treasures, ac-

24

Heinrich Karl Ernst Köhler. About 1800. Konstantin Afanasyev's engraving after a drawing by Franz Krüger. 28 × 22 cm. The Hermitage

quired by the Empress from Lanskoi's legatees after his death, later left the Museum. Rembrandt's *St Peter's Denial* and *Portrait of Titus* are now in Amsterdam and his *Alexander the Great*, in Lisbon. A beautiful collection of European 16th- to 18th-century bronzes which used to adorn Lanskoi's house on Palace Square also went to the Hermitage after his death, together with his miniatures, gems, glass copies of them and plaster casts, and jewellery objects. In 1777, Catherine received from Giuseppe Valadier in Rome a magnificent table ornament in rare coloured stones. But the late 18th-century Hermitage inventories contain no mention of it, nor of the author's book of drawings which had accompanied it. However, both objects eventually found their way to the Hermitage: the table ornament (minus the table itself, 2.40 m long) after Lanskoi's death, and the book of Valadier's watercolours in 1926. In 1782, Catherine commissioned a portrait of Lanskoi (now in the Russian Museum) from Dmitry Levitsky. It hung in her room in the Winter Palace to the day of her death, and in 1796 entered the Hermitage with the Empress's other cherished possessions. In 1827, Nicholas I ordered that the portrait of his grandmother's favourite should be removed from the Hermitage and rendered to Lanskoi's family. They, ashamed of the way in which Alexander Lanskoi rose into favour, exiled Levitsky's masterpiece to their country seat, where the noted collector, Prince Lobanov-Rostovsky, saw the portrait and bought it. Afterwards Nicholas II acquired it from the Prince's descendants, and the painting returned to the Hermitage after a century-long absence. In 1897, it was transferred to the Russian Museum.

Catherine II's taste in art was formed by her association with the leaders of the French Enlightenment and cultivated by years of practical collecting. Her opinions were close to those of the Neo-classicist Alexander Stroganov. Like him, she believed in "la composition sage, noble et grande", and while she was ready to agree with

Denis Diderot's view of Greuze's genre scenes from the life of the Third Estate, her conception of the representative dynastic portrait had more common with Baroque aesthetics. Evidence of this is provided by her own portrayals and the portrait series of European sovereigns commissioned by her for the Chesme Palace, and notably by the Empress's sharp criticism of the works by Elisabeth Vigée Lebrun, a French artist known as Peintre de Marie-Antoinette, who came to St Petersburg in 1796. She was met here with every show of cordiality and was showered with commissions for portraits of the aristocracy. The Empress too, through the mediation of Count Stroganov, ordered portrait of her two granddaughters Alexandra and Elena. In her *Memoirs*, the painter recorded that Catherine's favourite, Platon Zubov, informed her of the imperial patron's displeasure at the general style of the depiction and particularly at the girls' costumes. "The costumes were a little Greek," she admitted, "but very modest. I so believed in this gossip that I hastened to exchange the tunics for dresses such as princesses wear and cover the arms with boring long sleeves." Vigée Lebrun's assertions, however, have not been confirmed by X-ray examination of the canvas conducted by Inna Nemilova, Keeper of French Paintings at the Hermitage. It seems that the artist was ashamed to own that she did not paint from life but rather copied the first, rejected, version of the portrait, which she then destroyed like a guilty schoolgirl. The Empress's judgement of the second version is formulated with the utmost frankness in her letter to Grimm: "Madame Le Brun will squash the two figures down for you, there on a couch, twist the neck of the younger, give them the air of two pugs warming themselves in the sun, or if you wish of two unpleasant chimney-sweeps... The admirers of Mme Le Brun raise her on high, but this in my opinion is too bad, for this picture-portrait contains neither resemblance, nor taste, nor nobility... she should have copied Dame Nature and not invented some monkey poses."

25

It may be recalled in this connection that the Empress treated with great severity the wife of Grand Prince Alexander, who made her appearance at a ball in a dress which had been designed for her by Vigée Lebrun and which Catherine, without mincing her words, compared to a nightgown.

Having once adopted the Baroque view of dignity and grandeur as essential features of the state portrait, the Empress would not admit of any attempts at the lowering or simplification of the style.

The death of Catherine II in 1796 brought the first stage in the history of the Hermitage to a close. At this stage, it was the picture gallery that formed the foundation of the Museum, its principle section. A manuscript catalogue of paintings was compiled between 1773 and 1783 by Count Ernest Münnich. The first printed catalogue of the gallery (in French) appeared in 1774, and this was handed to visitors viewing the pictures. At present only three surviving copies of the catalogue are known.

Catherine II's collections also included miniatures, drawings, prints, numismatic and mineralogical cabinets, her cherished "antiques" (gems), minor bronzes, and jewellery objects numbering approximately 1,300 items. Notably, there were hardly any sculptures. Falconet's *Winter*, originally installed in the Hanging Garden of the Small Hermitage, did not remain there long. It was transferred to Gatchina; while the bulk of the Empress's collection of statuary was used to decorate her summer residence at Tsarskoye Selo.

Founded as a private museum, an ornament of the imperial palace, the Hermitage outgrew these narrow limits even before the close of Catherine's reign. We could search in vain for a single book of traveller's notes that did not contain a detailed description of its treasures as the most notable feature of the Palmyra of the North. In 1792, James Walker published in London two volumes of his own engravings after the best paintings of the Hermitage collection.

Catherine's rule was also associated with the accumulation of a rich stock of paintings contained in the private palaces of St Petersburg, many items from which later entered the Hermitage collections by various routes. Objects of applied and decorative art also poured in great number. Originally acquired for practical use, as articles necessary for the functioning of the imperial household, they came to form the basis of future collections of carriages, Gobelins, china, silverwork, etc.

Giovanni Battista Cipriani (1727–1785). Lucius Verus. 1760s. Drawing. British Museum, London

Lucius Verus. 2nd century. Marble. Height 76 cm. The Hermitage. From the Pavlovsk Palace collection

Catherine II acquired a magnificent collection of antique sculptures from the English banker Lyde Browne. Along with other sculptures, they formed the basis of the Hermitage collection of Roman portrait sculptures.

The Venus of Tauride. Roman copy of a Greek original (4th–3rd centuries B.C.). Marble. Height 169 cm. The Hermitage. From the Peter the Great collection

This statue of the goddess of love and beauty was inspired by the conception of the Aphrodite of Cnidus by Praxiteles. Later it was called the Venus of Tauride, after the Taurida Palace in St Petersburg, residence of Grigory Potiomkin, where it remained from the late 18th century until the mid-19th century.

Alvise Tagliapetra (active between 1697 and 1743). Justice. Marble. Height 202 cm. The Hermitage. From the Alexander Menshikov collection

Alvise Tagliapetra, a master of Baroque sculpture, was active in Venice. This statue was owned by Alexander Menshikov, Russian statesman, friend and chief adviser of Peter the Great, who held various governorships. The statue symbolizes the official valour of a governor.

Marie-Anne Collot (1748–1821). Portrait of Etienne Maurice Falconet. Marble. Height 45 cm. The Hermitage

Marie-Anne Collot, a pupil of Falconet, was herself a gifted sculptor, who executed, incidentally, the head of Peter the Great for Falconet's famous monument on Senate Square in St Petersburg (The Bronze Horseman).

Etienne Maurice Falconet (1716–1791). Cupid. 1766–69. Marble. Height 85 cm. The Hermitage. From the Alexander Bezborodko collection

Etienne Maurice Falconet began his artistic career at the Sèvres Porcelain Manufactory. Later, he used many of his miniature porcelain figurines as models for marble sculpture. Such was the case with Cupid.

Giorgione (1478?–1510). Judith.
Oil on canvas. 144 × 66.5 cm.
The Hermitage. From the Antoine
Crozat, Baron de Thiers,
collection, Paris

Paolo Veronese (1528–1588).
The Lamentation. Between 1576
and 1582. Oil on canvas.
147 × 111.5 cm. The Hermitage.
From the Antoine Crozat, Baron
de Thiers, collection, Paris

Garofalo (1481–1559).
The Entombment. 1520s. Oil on can-
vas. 53 × 75.5 cm. The Hermitage.
From the Peter the Great collection

Pieter Paul Rubens (1577–1640).
Christ Crowned with Thorns. About
1612. Oil on panel. 125.7 × 96.5 cm.
The Hermitage. From the Alexander
Bezborodko collection

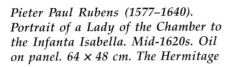

Pieter Paul Rubens (1577–1640).
Portrait of a Lady of the Chamber to
the Infanta Isabella. Mid-1620s. Oil
on panel. 64 × 48 cm. The Hermitage

Pieter Paul Rubens (1577–1640).
Perseus and Andromeda. Early
1620s. Oil on canvas. 99.5 × 139 cm.
The Hermitage. From the Heinrich
Brühl collection, Dresden

Jan Steen (1625/26–1679). Marriage
Contract. Early 1650s. Oil on can-
vas. 65 × 83 cm. The Hermitage.
From the Peter the Great collection

Hendrick Goltzius (1558–1617).
Bacchus, Venus and Ceres. Pen
drawing on canvas. 228 × 170 cm.
The Hermitage. From the Ivan
Betskoi collection

40

Frans Hals (1581/85–1666). Portrait of a Young Man with a Glove. About 1650. Oil on canvas. 80 × 66.5 cm. The Hermitage. From the Johann Ernest Gotzkowski collection, Berlin

Francisco de Zurbarán (1598–1664). The Crucifixion. 1650s. Oil on canvas. 265 × 173 cm. The Hermitage. From the Marble Palace, St Petersburg

Rembrandt Harmensz van Rijn (1606–1669). David Parting from Jonathan. 1642. Oil on panel. 73 × 61.5 cm. The Hermitage. From the Peter the Great collection

Rembrandt Harmensz van Rijn (1606–1669). Portrait of an Old Jew. 1654. Oil on canvas. 109 × 85 cm. The Hermitage. From the Alexander Lanskoi collection

Michiel Sweerts (1624–1664).
Self-portrait. 1656. Oil on canvas.
114 × 92 cm. The Hermitage. From
the Ivan Shuvalov collection

Louis Tocqué (1696–1772). Portrait
of Ivan Shuvalov. 1756–58. Oil on
canvas. 81 × 64 cm. The Hermitage.
From the Dmitry Tolstoi collection,
Petrograd

Johann-Baptist Lampi I (1751–1830).
Portrait of Prince Alexander Bez-
borodko. 1794. Oil on canvas.
121 × 95 cm. The Hermitage. From
the Alexander Bezborodko collection

Alessandro Magnasco (1667–1749).
The Halt of the Brigands. 1710s.
Oil on canvas. 112 × 162 cm.
The Hermitage. From the Ivan
Shuvalov collection

Heinrich Füger (1751–1818). Portrait
of Prince Nikolai Yusupov. Oil on
canvas. 112 × 87 cm. The Hermitage.
From Yusupov's palace

Richard Brompton (1734–1783).
Portrait of Crown Princes Alexander
and Constantine. Oil on canvas.
208 × 146 cm. The Hermitage.
From the Chesme Palace collection

Marie Louise Elisabeth Vigée
Lebrun (1755–1842). Portrait of
Paul I's Daughters. 1796. Oil on
canvas. 99 × 99 cm. The Hermitage

Joshua Reynolds (1723–1792).
The Continence of Scipio. 1788–89.
Oil on canvas. 239.5 × 165.5 cm.
The Hermitage. From the Grigory
Potiomkin collection

Joshua Reynolds (1723–1792). Cupid
Untying the Zone of Venus. 1788.
Oil on canvas. 127.5 × 101 cm.
The Hermitage. From the Grigory
Potiomkin collection

Jean-Baptiste Greuze (1725–1805).
Girl with a Doll. About 1757. Oil on
canvas. 65 × 55 cm. The Hermitage.
From the Ivan Shuvalov collection

Joshua Reynolds (1723–1792).
The Infant Hercules Killing Snakes.
1788. Oil on canvas. 303 × 297 cm.
The Hermitage. From the Catherine II
collection

Anton Raphael Mengs (1728–1779).
Perseus and Andromeda. 1777.
Oil on canvas. 227 × 153.5 cm.
The Hermitage

Konstantin Ukhtomsky (1818–1881).
Le Loggie in the Winter Palace. 1860.
Watercolour, lacquer. 42 × 25 cm.
The Hermitage

Cameo: Perseus and Andromeda.
1st century B.C. Agate. 2.8 × 3.1 cm.
The Hermitage. From the Catherine II
collection

The cameo of Perseus and Andromeda,
a masterpiece of "antique Rococo", as
the late Hellenistic period is sometimes
called, transforms an ancient myth into
a gallant scene. Hedonism, and even
explicit eroticism, is a characteristic
feature of the art of antique Rococo.
The cameo was purchased by Anton
Mengs in Spain. After his death, in
1779, Catherine II bought it together
with his own works.

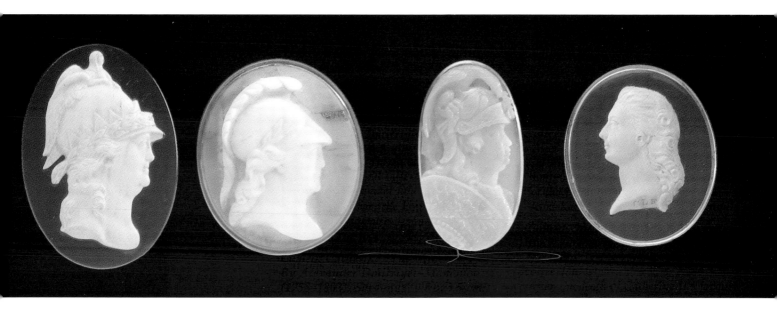

Cameo: Catherine II. By Grand
Princess Maria Fiodorovna. Sardonyx.
6.3 × 4.1 cm. The Hermitage

Maria Fiodorovna, Catherine's daughter-
in-law, executed portraits of her husband,
Crown Prince Paul (afterwards Paul I),
their sons, Alexander and Constantine,
and Catherine herself. This last won the
Empress's approval.

Cameo: Catherine II as Minerva.
By Alexander Dmitriyev-Mamonov
(1758–1803). Sardonyx. 4.8 × 3.5 cm.
The Hermitage. From the Catherine II
collection

Some people from the Empress's immediate entourage also began collecting
"antiques" or took up gem cutting technique. Alexander Dmitriyev-Mamonov
cut this portrait with his own hands.

Cameo: Grigory Potiomkin. By Georg
König (d. 1805). Sardonyx. 5 × 3.5 cm.
The Hermitage. From the Catherine II
collection

Catherine II commissioned from Georg
König several portraits of her favourite,
Grigory Potiomkin.

Cameo: Portrait of Alexander Lanskoi.
By Karl Leberecht (1755–1827).
Sardonyx. 3.8 × 2.8 cm. The Hermitage

After the death of Catherine II's favourite Alexander Lanskoi, the inconsolable
Empress commissioned several portraits
of the prematurely deceased general
from Karl Leberecht, stone carver and
engraver.

*Rhyton in the shape of a ram's head.
5th century B.C. Iran. Silver gilt.
Length 22 cm. The Hermitage.
From the Kunstkammer collection*

A superb silver rhyton in the shape of a
ram's head was produced in Persia under the Achaemenids. When housed in
the Kunstkammer, it was believed to
be a "Tatar military emblem".

*Monstrance. 1474. By Hans
Rissenberg. Revel. Silver gilt, glass.
Height 112 cm. The Hermitage.
From the Kunstkammer collection*

This magnificent silver monstrance was
kept in the Revel church of St Nicholas.
Afterwards the city council presented it
to Alexander Menshikov, who, in his
turn, gave it to Peter the Great.

*Dagger. 16th century. Italy. Ivory,
agate, silver gilt. Length 46 cm.
The Hermitage. From the Peter
the Great collection*

This dagger comes from a set of fine
blank weapons of various origin and
provenance. These splendidly ornamented daggers were wrought by armourers
of Iran, Turkey, Indonesia and Italy.
Peter the Great kept them in a special
casket in his private apartments.

Replica of Gianlorenzo Bernini's
La Fontana dei Quattro Fiume. Late
17th century. Silver. Height 42.3 cm.
The Hermitage. From the Kunstkam-
mer collection

The silver replica of Gianlorenzo Berni-
ni's "La Fontana dei Quattro Fiume"
was acquired for Peter the Great in Rome
in 1718. It entered the Kunstkammer as
a curio. Bernini's work is a copy of an
Egyptian obelisk which was brought to
Rome by Caracalla. Pope Innocent X put
it in Piazza Navona.

Giovanni da Bologna (1524–1608). Hercules and the Ceryneian Hind. Bronze. Height 40 cm. The Hermitage. From the Alexander Lanskoi collection

There were hardly any bronzes in the Hermitage until Catherine II's favourite Alexander Lanskoi died and his beautiful collection of bronzes came to the Hermitage. Among them was "Hercules and the Cyreneian Hind" by Giovanni da Bologna.

Unknown French sculptor active in the 18th century. The Death of Dido. Bronze. 96 × 53 cm. The Hermitage. From the Alexander Lanskoi collection

59

Russian Sovereigns. Early 18th century. By Johann Dorsch (1676–1732). Jasper. 3 × 2.5 cm. The Hermitage. From the James Bruce collection

Intaglio portraits on jasper feature a succession of Russian sovereigns from Prince Rurik to Tsar Ivan Alexeyevich. James Bruce, Peter the Great's companion-in-arms, commissioned this series from the Nuremberg gem cutter Johann Dorsch.

Ottmar Elliger (1666–1735). Cup of the Danish King. 1730s. Watercolour. 50 × 37 cm. The Hermitage. From the Kunstkammer collection

*Bunch of Flowers. By Jérémie Pauzier
(1716–1779). Gems. Height 19 cm.
The Hermitage*

Jérémie Pauzier was a jeweller to the
Russian court during the reign of three
Russian rulers: Elizabeth Petrovna,
Peter III and Catherine II. He designed
the crown for Catherine II's coronation.
He created attractive Baroque bouquets,
which were in fashion at that time, and
decorated them with varicoloured stones.
Ladies of the court used to pin such
bouquets onto their bodices. During the
reign of Catherine II Pauzier left Russia
and returned to his native Switzerland,
where he published his interesting
memoirs.

*Vase. Sèvres. Porcelain, bronze.
Height 190 cm. The Hermitage. From
the Alexander Bezborodko collection*

A masterpiece of the Sèvres Porcelain
Manufactory, this huge vase, decorated
with sculptural figures of putti, was
highly treasured by its original owner,
Prince Alexander Bezborodko. Several
travellers, who visited Russia's capital
in the late 18th century, mentioned
it in their memoirs as a unique work
of art.

The Chesme ink-pot. By Barnabé-Augustin de Mailly (1732–1793). Ormolu, ivory, enamel. 57.2 × 77 × 55 cm. The Hermitage. From the Catherine II collection

Fulfilling Catherine II's commission, Barnabé-Augustin de Mailly executed a real masterpiece of applied art. His ink-pot is decorated with scenes from the Russo-Turkish war as well as with playful cherubs typical of the French Rococo. This marvellous ink-pot was intended for the suburban Chesme Palace where knights of the order of St George held their meetings.

Giuseppe Valadier (1762–1839). Table Ornament. Watercolour. 27.5 × 44 cm. The Hermitage. From the Alexander Lanskoi collection

Eduard Hau (1807–about 1870). The Throne Room of Paul I on the Ground Floor in the Gatchina Palace. 1877. Watercolour. The Hermitage. From the Paul I collection

Clock: Cupid and Psyche. 1799. By Pierre Philippe Thomire (1751–1843). Ormolu. 86 × 85 × 28 cm. The Hermitage. From the Michael Castle collection

The splendid collection of clocks in the Michael Castle included the clock "Cupid and Psyche" made by Pierre Philippe Thomire in Paris. Legend has it that courtiers wishing to flatter their sovereign and to demonstrate how delighted they were with the clock's beauty fell on their knees before it. Another reason may have been that the images of Cupid and Psyche, figures from a late antique fairy tale, were often associated with Crown Prince Alexander and his wife Elizabeth.

Nicholas I, Founder of the New Hermitage

It was during the short reign of Paul I that the Hermitage first expanded beyond the limits of a purely private collection and developed certain features of an independent body. True, the Emperor still freely disposed of the Museum's holdings: thus, large numbers of pictures which he rightly considered as his own were removed to Paul's galleries at Pavlovsk and Gatchina; sculptures from Tsarskoye Selo were transferred to Gatchina and Pavlovsk; and the Emperor formed a completely new collection for the Michael Castle, his recently-built residence in St Petersburg. He bought only two important canvases for the Hermitage, Rubens's *The Union of Earth and Water* and Fragonard's *The Farmer's Children*. The rich collection of sculptures acquired by Paul in Venice from Farsetti went to the Academy of Arts and reached the Hermitage only as late as 1923. As for Catherine's cherished gems: on being told of the arrival of the next consignment of engraved stones from the London workshop of the Brothers Brown, Paul directed that for the future "no more of the kind be ordered".

But at the same time, whole series of canvases were commissioned from Paul's favourite painters, Jules Vernet and Hubert Robert, for the decoration of his summer residence, the Kamennoostrovsky Palace. Later, some of these paintings went to the Michael Castle and others, to Gatchina (now they are to be seen at the Hermitage and the Pavlovsk Palace Museum). Marble copies of famous antique statues were commissioned for the Michael Castle, whose decoration was carefully thought out by the Emperor himself, down to the smallest details. The ensemble of statuary, where copies alternated with ancient originals, reflected "the Russian Hamlet's" sense of tragedy and his abhorrence of his dead mother (Paolo Triscorni's *Cleopatra*, now in the Hermitage); and suggested a contrast between his former sufferings (*Laocoon*, *The Dying Gaul*, Roman funerary urns and sacrificial altars) and the ultimate triumph of order, beauty, harmony, and strength (*Apollo Belvedere*, *Diana of Versailles*, in the niches of the southern façade, *Hercules* and the *Farnese Flora*, in those of the northern front). The sculptural décor was echoed by pictorial decoration conveying, in the state rooms, a heroic, life-asserting mood (the Throne Room had monumental canvases by Ugriumov and Shebuyev — now in the Russian Museum), and in the private apartments, a sense of life's tragic aspects (Tiepolo's *The Feast of Cleopatra*, now at the Victoria Gallery, Melbourne; Vernet's *The Storm*, now in the Hermitage). Paul found room in his new residence for the gifts presented to him by the dethroned King Stanislas-Augustus of Poland: two sculptural groups symbolizing creative effort, commissioned in Rome from Pietro Staggio. One of them represented Pygmalion and Galatea, and the other, Prometheus creating Man (both now in the Hermitage). The artistic bronzes (clock cases, chandeliers, etc.) for the Michael Castle were ordered from the leading Parisian masters: Thomire and Gouthière.

As for the Hermitage, Paul's first care was to compile a complete inventory of its collections. The detailed list of paintings compiled in 1797 remained in use as the basic inventory of the Hermitage picture gallery for as long as fifty years!

After Paul I's death, all the art treasures assembled in his eccentric, new dwelling, which the Imperial family was destined to occupy for only forty days, left the shelter of the Michael Castle. The statues returned to Tsarskoye Selo and the Tauride Palace; while the paintings were divided among Gatchina, Pavlovsk, the Hermitage, and the Academy of Arts.

The accession of Alexander I brought a fresh atmosphere of new, liberal ideas and hopes of reform said to be in preparation among the young Emperor's circle of friends in his "Secret Committee". The spirit of change was felt in the Hermitage as well. In 1802, Count Dmitry Buturlin, a well-known art collector and bibliophile, was appointed Head of the Museum. He presented to the Tsar "a most humble petition" concerning the problems to be solved. This document pointed out the flaws in the composition of the picture gallery. As far as numbers go, said Buturlin, the gallery is second to none of the most celebrated world collections. But — as he argued with perfect justice — in the matter of paintings, quality should always take priority over numbers. It is true that even "the museum in Paris, enriched as it is with works imported from different parts of Europe ... does not own so rich and varied collections of paintings from the French and Dutch Schools". In Buturlin's opinion, "if we make good use of our opportunities to enlarge the collection of the Italian School (which has ever been the most difficult to assemble), ours will be the most outstanding in existence". Also, Buturlin suggested that the Hermitage be opened to the public "at a fixed season of the year, on condition that certain inviolable rules should be observed, and under the supervision of specially appointed staff". That was a sign of the times, and the Museum moved increasingly in the directions indicated by the Count; it was shifting farther and farther away from its beginnings as an exclusive private collection.

In 1808, Franz Labensky, Curator of the Picture Gallery, was sent on a mission to Paris. Vivant Denon, Director of the Musée Napoléon, was invited to co-operate with him in the work of complementing the Hermitage collection. The first acquisitions — two Caravaggios (his *Lute Player* and the *Martyrdom of St Peter*, now ascribed to the Caravaggist Lionello Spada) — were made in the famous Giustiniani Gallery; the rest was bought complete for the Berlin Museum in 1815. Alexander I authorized his Adjutant General Vladimir Trubetskoi and the diplomat Nikolai Khitrovo to acquire art works for him. In 1804, Khitrovo presented to him a marine by Jules Vernet and several hundred engraved gems, which made a welcome addition to the Hermitage collection. Yet it was the Tsar himself who scored the greatest success in the acquisition of art works. In 1814, while in Paris with the Russian army, he received as a gift from the former Empress Josephine Beauharnais one of the most far-famed gems of antiquity, the celebrated Gonzaga cameo. Josephine also owned forty-eight canvases from the collection of the Landgrave of Cassel, which had come into her hands during Napoleonic wars and which she had placed in her gallery at Malmaison Castle. Vivant Denon who, in his turn, had carried away from Cassel three hundred pictures for the Louvre, vainly tried to add to them the Malmaison paintings: Napoleon had given them as a present to his divorced wife. In 1814, Josephine suddenly died. Alexander I bought the paintings from her legatees, adding four Canova sculptures to the deal, for 940,000 francs. His ally, the Landgrave of Cassel, wished to have his pictures back; yet Alexander agreed to return them only on condition that his expenses be refunded. As might be expected, the Landgrave refused, saying that it was not his intention to pay twice for his own pictures.

As a result of this transaction, the Hermitage was enriched with Andrea del Sarto's *The Holy Family*, Lorrain's series of *The Times of the Day*, several magnificent paintings by Rembrandt, Potter, Gerard Terborch, Gabriel Metsu, and Flemish canvases by David Teniers and Rubens — the finest pearls of the Cassel collection. This was always remembered at Cassel. In 1817, the Russian painter Orest Kiprensky, on a visit to Cassel, heard his guide complain that the best pictures had been carried away to Malmaison. "Now, thank God, they have moved to Bellemaison and adorn the Hermitage."

Almost at the same time Alexander I bought the Amsterdam collection of the English banker William Coesvelt, enriching the Spanish section of the Hermitage, hitherto one of the weakest, with a number of important canvases by such great artists as Diego Velásquez, Francisco de Zurbarán, and Antonio Pereda. This greatly contributed to the development of the Spanish collection.

The most striking innovation of Alexander's reign was the creation of a department of Russian painting.

Stepan Shchukin (1762–1828). Portrait of Paul I. Oil on canvas. 154 × 116 cm. The Hermitage

Catherine II had owned only two canvases of the Russian School: Anton Losenko's *Vladimir and Rogneda* and his *Miraculous Draught of Fishes* (now in the Russian Museum). From 1802 onwards, the Hermitage came to possess works by Andrei Martynov, Fiodor Alexeyev, Fiodor Matveyev, Vasily Shebuyev, Alexei Egorov, and other native artists.

In 1824, Vasily Grigorovich addressed the Empress with a memorandum concerning "the desirability of having a special department of works by Russian painters formed in the Hermitage". The memorandum met with august approbation. The Tsar ordered a complete list of Russian paintings housed in the palaces of St Petersburg and Moscow to be drawn up, and a few months later, a picture gallery of the Russian School was founded in the Hermitage. It functioned until 1898 when the collection was transferred to the newly-established Russian Museum. The setting up of the department strengthened further the links between Russian artists and the Museum. Keepers for the gallery were recruited from among the Academy staff, such as Professors Mikhail Ivanov and Alexander Varnek, Fiodor Bruni and Timofei Neff. The Russian painter Alexei Venetsianov, when working on his *Threshing Floor*, wrote in a letter from his estate to St Petersburg, how he cherished a hope of having his picture accepted for the Hermitage gallery of the Russian School. "I have no greater desire than to be represented there on the same wall as Granet." Another prominent Russian master, Karl Briullov, was , as a young man, an ardent admirer of the Hermitage. Taras Shevchenko, artist and poet, recalled how Briullov, showing the treasures of the Hermitage to his class, would always finish his lecture in front of David Teniers's *The Guard Room* (one of the Malmaison pictures) and "after a warm and enthusiastic tribute to the great Fleming, would say, 'To see this painting alone is worth coming over from America!'"

With the accession of Nicholas I in 1825, the Hermitage entered the next important phase of its history. The new Emperor himself was no stranger to the visual arts. He had studied painting under Alexander Sauerweid, Professor of the Academy of Arts. The Empress Alexandra Fiodorovna mentioned in her memoirs how, in the winter of 1819, then living in the Anichkov Palace, the Grand Prince Nicholas "used to give much of his time to painting military subjects". The result of his efforts was a series of dry, rigid figures of cavalry and infantry soldiers, preserved up to 1917 in the Imperial Library of the Hermitage. A still more specific use of the Emperor's painterly skills appears in his catalogue of pictures in his private possession. Of the 666 canvases decorating His Majesty's private suite, 650 represented figures in military uniforms. Here is one of the entries in the catalogue: "Landscape of the Flemish School, with Russian cavalry soldiers in the foreground... Van Goyen. Landscape. Manoeuvre of the Russian Troops. Figures painted by H. I. M. as Grand Prince..."

In his judgement on the merits of individual painters, Nicholas relied on his natural taste. Painters of battle scenes strongly appealed to him. He set the highest value on Horace Vernet, whose picture *French Guards on Parade* elicited from the Emperor the following order: "This painting is to remain in my study. I want to have the French Guards constantly before my eyes: for they might have defeated us." This was an allusion to the turning point of the battle at Borodino when Napoleon shrank from sacrificing his guards.

Nicholas I commissioned from the Munich artist Peter Hess a series of pictures showing some of the battles in the 1812 War. He commented on the canvas *The Battle of Viazma* in a letter sent to Munich in 1842: "1. The officers' coats in the picture are buttoned down the left front; our officers all button theirs down the right front. 2. The cloak of a non-commissioned officer should not have galloon. 3. No white edging to the cravat."

Soon after his accession, it fell to Nicholas I to celebrate the completion of the grandiose project started by his

George Dawe (1781–1829). Portrait of Alexander I. Oil on canvas. 238 × 152.3 cm. The Hermitage

predecessor: on 25 December 1826, the ceremonial opening of the 1812 War Gallery took place. Its 333 portraits of generals, who had commanded the Russian army in the Napoleonic Wars of 1812–14, were painted in the St Petersburg workshop of the English portraitist George Dawe. The celebration was somewhat clouded by the young monarch's command that the pictures of those involved in the Decembrists' revolt should be taken down. In his commentary to the *Memoirs* of the widow of Decembrist General Sergei Volkonsky the latter's grandson tells us, that "the portrait of Prince Sergei Volkonsky, placed in the Gallery of the generals of the Patriotic War in the Winter Palace, was excluded from it in 1826 by H.I.M.'s command; found in one of the palace storerooms, it was restored to its place in 1903, seventy-seven years later..."

Alexander Pushkin described the Gallery in inspired verse:

The Tsar's great palace has a lofty hall:
No velvet, gold, upon the royal wall,
Nor jewels under glass in casket glow;
But where'er one's glance may turn, above, below,
The painter's hand declares with faultless candour
A man's bold brush, his art of magic splendour.
No buxom women, sylvan nymphs, nor maids,
No fauns with brimming bowls, no forest glades,
Nor hunting scenes, — only uniforms and swords
And faces stern before their warring hordes,
Here, painted on the walls, a galaxy
Of chiefs who gave their land their mastery
In war, and crowned their lives with fadeless glory
In Eighteen-Twelve, in Russian fame and story.
I've mused in silence here for many days.
Before each canvas long I love to gaze
And dream. I hear on battle-fields in war
Their voices ring...

Translated by Eugene M. Kayden

When artistic and historical relics from Poland, confiscated after the suppression of the Warsaw uprising of 1831, arrived in St Petersburg, Nicholas I ordered that they be destroyed. We have at our present disposal a report by the Hermitage restorer, Alexander Mitrokhin, addressed to Franz Labensky, Curator of the Picture Gallery, to the following effect: "In fulfilment of Your Excellency's instructions of this 26 July concerning the destruction, by H.I.Majesty's command, of certain portraits, pictures, and other things brought from Warsaw in seventeen boxes, we have the honour to report that this 31 July... the said portraits, pictures, and other things have been annihilated and burnt, with the exception of a portrait of the Emperor Alexander I which we intend to rub out with pomice stone..." There was but a single object that escaped being destroyed by this act of vandalism: Vasily Zhukovsky begged from the Emperor, for his own collection, a portrait of his brother writer, the poet Julian Niemcewicz, and was allowed to take it. This work, thus miraculously saved, is an example of the art of Antoni Brodowski (now in the National Museum, Warsaw).

And yet it can hardly be averred that Nicholas had no understanding of art. He had, but the boundless conceit of the autocrat was apt to cloud his judgement. This is well illustrated by a characteristic remark cited by Fiodor Bruni: "Considering my position in the state, I should be the country's first artist." We know how art scholars were divided in their opinions of the marble sculptures by Phidias brought from Athens by Lord Elgin and placed on exhibition in the British Museum in London. Some thought that they were the work of "the ablest artists the world had ever seen" and were far superior to all the treasures of Italy; while others saw them as routine productions from the Roman epoch. Greatly to the credit of Nicholas, after his visit to London in 1817 he praised the Elgin Marbles to the sky in a conversation with Alexei Olenin, President of the Academy of Arts; moreover, he presented Olenin with engravings of the famous sculp-

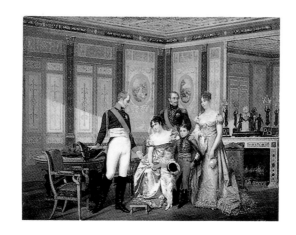

Hector Viger (1819–1879).
Alexander I in Malmaison.
Oil on canvas. Malmaison

tures which he had bought on the journey. This gave Olenin the idea of buying plaster casts of the Elgin Marbles for the St Petersburg Academy of Arts.

It is customary for authors dealing with the period in question to dwell upon Nicholas I's "persecution" of the Houdon statue of Voltaire, his order for the destruction of art objects brought from Poland after the insurrection of 1831, and his resolute purging of the Hermitage collections of relics associated with the favourites of his grandmother, Catherine II. But each of these actions was dictated by considerations of a purely political nature. And it would be only fair to balance it against the sum of all the good done by Nicholas I for the Hermitage, from the building of the New Museum to extensive acquisitions of masterpieces for its collections.

The idea of building a New Hermitage originated and matured after the urgent restoration of the Winter Palace, gutted by the great fire of 1837. It was a logical outcome of the recognition of the many problems of the Museum, which was growing like a living organism. Also, it fitted in with the contemporary tendency in the development of European museums. After the fall of Napoleon in 1814, European collections entered on a period of vigorous growth, which led to their gradual transformation into public museums. In 1816, the British government acquired the Parthenon sculptures; in 1814, Ludwig I, the future king of Bavaria, bought the Aegina marbles and, in 1815, the Albani collection of antique sculptures. In 1830, the architect Leo von Klenze completed the construction of the Glyptothek in Munich, which was to receive these treasures; and in 1836, the Munich Pinakothek, another of his museum buildings, was opened. In 1830, Karl Schinkel finished his New Museum in Berlin, which became known as the Old Museum after 1843, when his pupils built the New Museum. The need for Russia to have a museum which might house, in addition to a picture gallery, collections of sculptures and archaeological finds, was becoming more and more pressing. Excavations of Scythian barrows in the Black Sea coast area showed that immense treasures were to be found not only in Siberia but also in the Crimea. Following the successful excavations of the barrows, archaeologists started diggings on the sites of antique towns located in the area. The results caused a veritable sensation.

Nicholas I's choice of Leo von Klenze as designer for the new museum was not fortuitous. In 1838, while in Munich, he had seen both the Glyptothek and the Pinakothek, with the architect himself as his guide. It was then that a design for the New Hermitage was commissioned from Klenze. In 1839, he was invited to come to St Petersburg, and building works were begun according to his design.

The royal patron and the architect agreed that the Museum itself should be a work of art. Rich polychromy, the use of costly finishing materials, façade decorations including sculptural portraits of artists and other devices, not always functionally justified in a building intended to serve museum purposes, made Nicholas I's New Hermitage an ornament to his capital. The granite columns and sculptures; the vases of porphyry, lapis lazuli, and rhodonite; the walls faced with shining stucco looking for all the world like marble; the gilt bronze and precious kinds of wood all combined to create an effect of festive, enchanting beauty. Completed in 1850, the Museum was opened to the public in 1852. A marble plaque on its grand staircase reads: "Erected by the Emperor Nicholas I in 1850." There is a tradition that shortly before his death, crushed by Russia's defeat in the Crimean War and the collapse of her might, the Tsar, seeing again his darling child, the New Hermitage, after months of absence, was heard to utter these meaningful words, "Yes: here is perfection indeed!" He deserves credit not only as the initiator and inspirer of the creation of the new museum, but also as a painstaking and scrupulous participant in the work of the arrangement of its collections. Fiodor Bruni, appointed Director of the Picture Gallery, wrote in his

73

Franz Krüger (1797–1857). Portrait of Nicholas I. 1852. Oil on canvas. 93 × 72 cm. The Hermitage

Memoirs that every day, from 13 to 14 o'clock, the Emperor would come to supervise the work of the commission engaged in the selection and hanging of pictures. "If he had once defined a painting as a work of this or that school, it was no easy matter to make him change his opinion: 'This is Flemish.' 'But it seems to me, Your Majesty...' 'No, Bruni, don't you argue. Flemish it is!' " In 1851, Nicholas I made the following entry in the text of the Regulations compiled by Bruni: "The original arrangement is determined by H.M. the Emperor." It was only now, under Nicholas I, that the practice of hanging canvases close together so as to achieve an overall "tapestry" effect, in use since as far back as Catherine's reign, was finally abandoned. However, in the Regulations of 1851 "symmetrical arrangement" is still recommended as preferable, "but only in cases where it can be effected without detriment to the historically justified grouping of the works."

All this would have been fine but for one aspect of Nicholas I's personality: his blind faith in his innate infallibility as a bearer of sovereign power. A commission comprising three painters, Bruni, Piotr Basin, and Neff, was empowered to decide the fate of the Hermitage's paintings. The 4,552 pictures were divided into four classes: 1) those meant for display in the Gallery (815); 2) those fit to serve as decoration of the imperial palaces (804); 3) those to be put in store (1,369), and 4) those of no importance (1,564).

Works of the fourth class, which failed to qualify as possessing any artistic value, were examined in the Tauride Palace by the Emperor himself. He had some of them sent away to various institutions in the capital, and others given to his family and courtiers. The remaining 1,219 were sold at auction. In March 1854, this deplorable sale took place. The net profit came to 16,500 roubles, each individual picture fetching on average less than 14 roubles! The responsibility for this absurd transaction falls on Nicholas I; but in the matter of selection and classifica-

tion of the canvases it is shared by the painters who were on the commission. Ernest Münnich, the compiler of Catherine I's catalogue, had shown far greater knowledge, understanding and artistic sense than did Fiodor Bruni eighty years later.

Chardin's *Still-life with Attributes of the Arts* returned to the Hermitage, but only after the 1917 revolution, in 1926. Charles Natoire's *Cupid Sharpening an Arrow* arrived from Kiev in 1932. Pieter Lastman's *Abraham on the Road to Canaan* was bought for the Museum in 1938. The wings of Lucas van Leyden's triptych, sold in 1854 for 30 roubles, were recovered in 1885 for 8,000 roubles. Some of the auctioned canvases went abroad and were incorporated in foreign collections: *St Jerome* by José Ribera is now in Warsaw; *Joseph Carreras* by Godfrey Kneller, in London; *The Music Lesson* by Gerard Terborch, in Philadelphia, USA.

The sale of the Hermitage pictures once acquired with the collections of Crozat, Brühl, and Walpole was an event by no means exceptional in museum practice of the time. In 1913, Nikolai Wrangel referred to it as an example of "epidemic barbarism". In 1852, 1,000 paintings were sold from Munich Pinakothek for 6,000 guilders. In 1856, in Budapest, 300 canvases went for 700 florins. The idea was probably suggested to Nicholas I by sales like these.

And there was some compensation, for during Nicholas' reign, additions to the Hermitage picture gallery were made on a particularly large scale. In 1831, the Spanish section was considerably enriched by the purchase of paintings from the collection of the Madrid Minister of State, Manuel de Godoy, then living in exile. In 1850, the entire collection of the Palazzo Barbarigo, where Titian died, was acquired in Venice. The paintings, assembled as far back as the 16th century, included several works by Titian himself, referred to with great admiration by the Renaissance historian Carlo Ridolfi in his *Le Meraviglie dell'arte* (1643). All the Hermitage Titians except

*Eduard Hau (1807 – about 1870).
Room of the Russian School
of Painting in the New
Hermitage. 1856. Watercolour.
29 × 46.9 cm. The Hermitage*

Danaë and *The Flight into Egypt* come from the Palazzo Barbarigo. Also in 1850, Bruni was sent to The Hague to attend a sale of paintings belonging to the collection of King William II of the Netherlands. The acquisitions made by the agent of the Russian Tsar were widely discussed in the press. Bruni bought some Old Master canvases of the Italian School, such as *Columbine (Portrait of a Woman)* by Francesco Melzi, then ascribed to Leonardo, Sebastiano del Piombo's *Deposition* and Guercino's *Martyrdom of St Catherine*. But his attention was mainly concentrated on works by Netherlandish artists of the 15th century, necessary to fill the lacunae in the Hermitage collection. So he bought *The Descent from the Cross* by Jan Gossaert, *The Glorification of the Virgin* by Jan Provost, and *St Luke Drawing a Portrait of the Virgin* by Rogier van der Weyden, or rather its right-hand portion: the original picture having been sawn in two; its left-hand portion was acquired later, in 1884.

Shortly after the opening of the New Hermitage in the spring of 1852, Bruni went to Paris where a sale was to be held of the Soult collection. Soult, one of Napoleon's marshals, amassed during his Spanish campaign a number of important paintings of the Spanish School. Bruni dreamed of buying the pearl of Soult's collection, Bartolomé Esteban Murillo's *Immaculate Conception*, although the Hermitage already owned an analogous composition acquired with the Walpole collection. But the limited sum allotted for his purchases fell far short of the amount needed to outbid the agents of the Louvre, who finally got the canvas. By way of compensation, the Hermitage Director bought Murillo's *Liberation of St Peter* and Francisco de Zurbarán's *St Lawrence*.

Nicholas himself also bought pictures. In 1820, as Crown Prince, he acquired in Dresden Caspar David Friedrich's *On a Sailing Boat*, which entered the Hermitage gallery at a later date from the Peterhof palace called The Cottage. Another picture by Friedrich, *The Dreamer (Ruins of the Oybin Monastery)* — now in the

Hermitage — was in the Empress's study in the Anichkov Palace. It seems that the canvases and drawings of the Dresden artist were acquired through the mediation of the poet Vasily Zhukovsky who was personally acquainted with him. Thus, in 1821 Zhukovsky wrote to Empress Alexandra Fiodorovna: "I found in his (i.e. Friedrich's) studio several unfinished pictures; one of them you might possible like to have — it would match a canvas you have already; it shows a return to their homeland of those seen leaving it in your picture." The painting in question is the Hermitage canvas *Moonrise over the Sea*, which came to the Museum from the Ropsha Palace.

Nicholas I purchased paintings by Orest Kiprensky and Karl Briullov — some for his private collection, others for the Russian section at the Hermitage, where pride of place belonged to two monumental works, Karl Briullov's *Last Day of Pompeii*, and Fiodor Bruni's *Brazen Serpent* (both now in the Russian Museum). The gem collections, once the glory of Catherine II's Hermitage, were continually enlarged by new accessions. The façade of the New Hermitage, decorated by Klenze such as to give the viewer an idea of the Museum's most treasured possessions, bears a bas-relief of the Genius of the Glyptic Art, and sculptures of the two most famous gem cutters of antiquity, Pyrgoteles and Dioskourides.

In 1831, the gem collection confiscated from the Polish archaeologist Kazimerz Weselowsky was brought to St Petersburg from Warsaw. In 1851, Princess Eudoxia Golitsyna bequeathed to Nicholas I a Hellenistic cameo with the head of Zeus. But the most remarkable and the richest gift was that of the diplomat Dmitry Tatishchev. He died in Vienna in 1845, leaving to the Emperor all his art collections: fine urns, sculptures, mosaics, and paintings. The latter included masterpieces of the Spanish and Netherlandish Schools, among them diptychs by Jan van Eyck (now in the Metropolitan Museum of Art, New York), and two wings of a diptych by Robert Campin (now in the Hermitage); also canvases by Jan Provost and

Adriaen Isenbrandt. But perhaps the most remarkable part of the Tatishchev bequest was his dactyliothek, a rare ensemble which has been preserved intact. It is a portable casket decorated with gems on the outside and containing within 141 engraved gems in precious settings. The gems included some specimens of Greek, Italic, and Roman work, and creations of Renaissance glyptic artists; but the greater part were by masters of Neo-classicism, no less than eighteen signed by Pichler himself.

Nicholas I was sensible to the beauty of ancient art and felt an interest in classical archaeology. He initiated a perfectly unparalleled project, commissioning Leo von Klenze to design for the New Hermitage a gallery dedicated to the history of ancient painting. A somewhat similar idea had been explored by the architect in his Munich Pinakothek, where he used in the decoration some subjects from the history of Italian and German painting. But in the New Hermitage, the approach to the theme was to be different. It was to be based on the concept of the continuity of artistic traditions in Classical, Byzantine, and Russian painting. According to the original plan, the Anteroom leading to the gallery was to be painted with six frescoes tracing the tradition from St Olga, bringing Byzantine icons to the land of Rus, to the Empress Elizabeth Petrovna, founding the Academy of Arts. Later the plan was abandoned in favour of another project: to devote the Anteroom to paintings of the Russian School. The sketches for the frescoes executed by Piotr Basin have survived and are now in the Russian Museum, but they were long misinterpreted and their original purpose forgotten. Eighty-six watercolour sketches for the Gallery were painted in Munich by Georg Hiltensperger; and by 1848 the pictures themselves, eighty in number, arrived in St Petersburg. They were painted on copper and were intended to revive the encaustic technique — using colours mixed with wax — practised in antiquity.

In 1845, Nicholas I made a voyage to Naples on board the steamship *Kamchatka*. In honour of the august visit, special excavations were staged in the presence of the Tsar. All the finds were presented by the King of Naples to Nicholas and afterwards placed in the Hermitage. They included a bronze steelyard with the counterpoise shaped as a miniature portrait of Caligula, a marble group of a boy with a bird, and other objects.

In 1840, before his Neapolitan journey, Nicholas I visited Kerch. Here, too, he received some gifts of finds made — supposedly by chance — in the burial of a woman described as the Masked Queen (really the tomb of Bosporan King Rheskuporis). The ignorant but quick-witted officials presented to the Tsar the traditional bread-and-salt of welcome on a silver plate of "the queen". Later on, in 1851, two marble sculptures found in the Kerch area came to the Hermitage. Nicholas founded the Imperial Archaeological Commission and ordered a room in the Hermitage to be given over to house antiquities from the Cimmerian Bosporus, in addition to the so-called Cabinet of the Empress where gold and silver objects from South Russia were on display.

Not a little care was given by the Emperor to the formation and development of the Hermitage collection of antique sculptures. It was based on statuary transferred here from the Tauride Palace and Tsarskoye Selo. In 1851, the Demidov collection was bought in St Petersburg; it consisted of twenty-four pieces of sculpture, including some rare large-scale portraits of Roman emperors, executed in the 2nd century. A year later, fifty-four sculptures and 330 vases were acquired for the Hermitage from the Laval family. As far back as 1826, in the early period of his reign, Nicholas purchased from Ivan Laval's son-in-law, the Austrian ambassador Count Lebzeltern, his collection of classic sculptures. Ludwig Lebzeltern, the owner, having been implicated in the Decembrists' affair, had to leave for Vienna with all speed.

For the first time since Shuvalov's days, purchases of antique sculptures in Italy were resumed. To this end, an Archaeological Commission for the acquisition of antiquities was established in Rome, with Prince Grigory Volkonsky at the head. Stepan Gedeonov (later Director of the Hermitage) was appointed his assistant. The Commission was to conduct excavations, and a piece of land on the Palatine Hill was bought for the purpose. However, in 1851, Pope Pius IX offered several sculptures from papal museums in exchange for it, and his offer was accepted. In the same year, Gedeonov bought in Venice three important antique sculptures from the collection of Senator Nani: *Apollo, Alexander*, and *Aphrodite*; and two more, *Hyacynth* and a *Caryatid*, from the Soranzo and Algarotti palaces.

The acquisition of a small collection of Egyptian antiquities led to the foundation of a special section. The new accessions, formerly owned by Nicholas I's son-in-law, Duke Maximilian von Leuchtenberg, included such important items as some granite sarcophagi and a basalt sculpture of Arsinoë II.

Two more new sections, formed on the initiative of the Tsar, were housed in the galleries flanking the pavilion of Vallin de la Mothe in Catherine I's Small Hermitage: the portrait gallery of the house of the Romanovs (in the western gallery) and the Gallery of Peter the Great, together with a Gallery of Objects de vertu (in the eastern gallery). In 1848, the Gallery of Peter the Great was enriched by numerous articles transferred from the Petrine *Kunstkammer*. The Peacock Clock wrought by James Cox, once an item of Grigory Potiomkin's collection in the Tauride Palace, was placed in the centre of the Gallery of Objects de vertu.

Under Nicholas I, the beginnings were laid of the practice of recording, in watercolour drawings, the interiors of the New Hermitage and the exhibitions arranged in them. The work was executed by the artists Konstantin Ukhtomsky, Eduard Hau, and Luigi Premazzi. A veritable memorial of Nicholas I's reign was created by the publication of a luxury edition, in three volumes, of *Antiquities from the Cimmerian Bosporus*, which came out in 200 copies in 1854. It was illustrated with drawings by René Picard and Fiodor Solntsev and engravings by Picard, Konstantin Afanasyev, Kozma Chesky, Dmitry Andrussky, and Vasily Semechkin. Some forty years later, in 1892, the well-known French archaeologist Salomon Reinach published a repeat edition, in reduced size, of this rare work, now owned only by the world's largest libraries.

The Emperor created another museum in his country residence at Tsarskoye Selo, an exclusive, private affair, known as The Arsenal. This contained rare arms from the Petrine *Kunstkammer*, specimens of armour from the Tatishchev collection, Venetian guns from the collection of Maximilian von Leuchtenberg, Oriental arms and armour received as diplomatic gifts, Russian arms and armour from the Mikhail Pogodin collection, and other rarities of a like nature. Eventually these treasures were to find their way to the Hermitage.

To sum up, the history of the Hermitage in the first half of the 19th century was marked by Nicholas I's vigorous activity in museum building and collecting. Except for the unfortunate sale of 1854 and certain individual acts of vandalism, prompted by the political passions of the time, this aspect of the Emperor's statesmanship was highly successful. Russia came to have a public museum of the universal type, perfectly up-to-date in its structure and arrangements, and incorporating the former private collections of Catherine II's Hermitage, the Tauride Palace, and other imperial palaces.

78

Andrea del Sarto (1486–1531).
The Holy Family. 1519. Oil on canvas.
102 × 80 cm. The Hermitage. From
the Empress Josephine collection,
Malmaison Castle near Paris

Jan Gossaert (about 1478–1532).
The Descent from the Cross. 1521.
Oil on canvas. 141 × 106.5 cm.
The Hermitage. From the collection
of King William II of the Nether-
lands, The Hague

82

Titian (1485/90–1576). The Penitent
Maria Magdalene. 1560s. Oil on
canvas. 118 × 97 cm. The Hermitage.
From the Barbarigo collection, Venice

Caravaggio (1571–1610). The Lute
Player. About 1595. Oil on canvas.
94 × 119 cm. The Hermitage. From
the Giustiniani collection, Paris

Lucas van Leyden (1489/94–1533).
The Healing of the Blind Man
of Jericho. Triptych. 1531.
Oil on canvas.

115.5 × 150.5 cm (central part);
89 × 33.5 cm (wings). The Hermitage.
From the Antoine Crozat, Baron de
Thiers, collection, Paris

Pieter Paul Rubens (1577–1640).
The Descent from the Cross. About
1618. Oil on canvas. 297 × 200 cm.
The Hermitage. From the Empress
Josephine collection, Malmaison
Castle near Paris

Pieter Lastman (1583–1633).
Abraham on the Road to Canaan.
1614. Oil on canvas. 72 × 122 cm.
The Hermitage

Francisco de Zurbarán (1598–1664).
St Lawrence. 1636. Oil on canvas.
292 × 225 cm. The Hermitage. From
the Marshal Soult collection, Paris

Velásquez (1599–1660). Portrait of
Count Olivarez. About 1640. Oil on
canvas. 67 × 54.5 cm. The Hermitage.
From the William Coesvelt collection, Amsterdam

88

4135

Claude Lorrain (1600–1682).
Noon. 1651 or 1661. Oil on canvas.
113 × 157 cm. The Hermitage. From
the Empress Josephine collection,
Malmaison Castle near Paris

Paulus Potter (1625–1654). Watch-
dog. Oil on canvas. 96.5 × 132 cm.
The Hermitage. From the Empress
Josephine collection, Malmaison
Castle near Paris

Gerard Terborch (1617–1681).
A Glass of Lemonade. Oil on canvas.
67 × 54 cm. The Hermitage. From
the Empress Josephine collection,
Malmaison Castle near Paris

David Teniers the Younger (1610–1654). Monkeys in the Kitchen. Oil on canvas. 36 × 50.5 cm. The Hermitage. From the Empress Josephine collection, Malmaison Castle near Paris

92

Charles Joseph Natoire (1700–1777).
Cupid Sharpening an Arrow. 1750.
Oil on canvas. 55.5 × 42.5 cm. The
Hermitage. From the Antoine Crozat,
Baron de Thiers, collection, Paris

Jean-Baptiste Siméon Chardin (1699–
1779). Still Life with Attributes of
the Arts. 1766. Oil on canvas.
112 × 140.5 cm. The Hermitage

96

Claude Joseph Vernet (1714–1789).
The Storm. Oil on canvas.
152 × 204 cm. The Hermitage.
From the Paul I collection

François Gérard (1770–1837).
Portrait of Josephine Beauharnais.
1801. The Hermitage. From the Duke
of Leuchtenberg collection

Jean-Baptiste Greuze (1725–1805).
Curé's Visit. 1786. Oil on canvas.
126 × 160.5 cm. The Hermitage.
From the Paul I collection

Caspar David Friedrich (1774–1840).
*The Dreamer (Ruins of the Oybin
Monastery). Oil on canvas.
27 × 21 cm. The Hermitage.
From the Nicholas I collection*

Caspar David Friedrich (1774–1840).
*On a Sailing Boat. Oil on canvas.
71 × 56 cm. The Hermitage. From
the Nicholas I collection*

101

Intaglio: The Nymph Aura.
1st century B.C. Dioskourides'
workshop. Amethyst.
3.5 × 3 cm. The Hermitage.
From the Alexander I collection

The nymph Aura, symbolizing propitious breeze, was especially popular during the reign of the Roman Emperor Augustus. Aura was believed to fill out the sails of Roman ships and thus help Augustus to defeat the fleet of Mark Antony and Cleopatra.

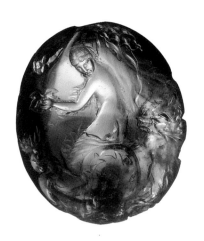

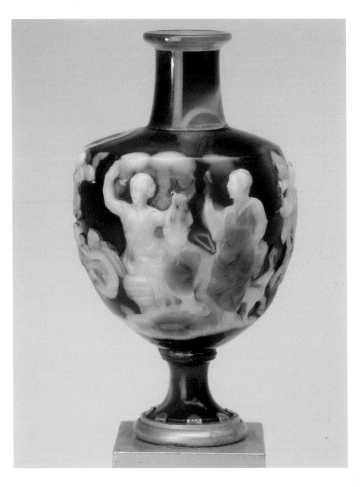

Amphora: Triumph of Love.
1st century. Rome. Sardonyx.
Height 5.5 cm. The Hermitage.
From the Alexander I collection

This rare miniature amphora (amphoriskos) carved from sardonyx in the cameo technique represents the type of vessel which Horace described as "a tiny onyx filled with nard". During the Renaissance the amphora belonged to the collection of Francis I of France at Fontainebleau.

Cameo: Ptolemy II and Arsinoë ("Gonzaga cameo"). 3rd century B.C. Sardonyx. 15.7 × 11.8 cm. The Hermitage. Gift of the Empress Josephine to Alexander I

The rulers of Hellenistic Egypt, Ptolemy II Philadelphus and his wife Arsinoë, are represented here as gods of the Greek Pantheon. The cameo's history can be traced from 1542, when it was first mentioned in the inventories of the Gonzagas, Dukes of Mantua.

Cameo: Constantine the Great and the Tyche of Constantinople. 4th century. Rome. Sardonyx. 18.5 × 12.2 cm. The Hermitage. From the Nikolai Khitrovo collection

This cameo was known under the erroneous name of "the Trajan cameo". Actually, it was carved much later, in the 4th century, during the decline of the old world of antiquity. In the late 18th century, it was substantially reworked.

104

Head of a Satyr. Roman copy of a 3rd-century B.C. original. Marble. Height 30 cm. The Hermitage. From the Paul I collection in Gatchina

Portrait of Balbinus. 3rd century. Marble. Height 72.5 cm. The Hermitage. From the Laval collection

In the history of Rome the 3rd century was known as "an epoch of soldiers' emperors". It was the time when the Praetorian Guards constantly changed the rulers of the Empire. In 238, soldiers put on the throne the young Gordian III, who was still under age. The Senate appointed Balbinus and Putinus as Gordian's co-rulers, but both were soon assassinated. The sculptor here strove not only to reveal the model's inner world but the spirit of the age in which he lived.

Antonius Pius. 2nd century. Marble. Height 224 cm. The Hermitage. From the P. Demidov collection

This statue of Antonius Pius was discovered in Rome in 1825 during the excavations conducted by the Russian mine-owner Nikolai Demidov.

Relief with bucrania. 1st century. Marble. Height 87 cm. The Hermitage. From the Michael Castle collection

Paul I ordered that the Roman sarcophagi should be transferred from Tsarskoye Selo to the Antique Hall on the first

floor of the Michael Castle. A relief with bucrania imparted to the interior an atmosphere of a funeral feast.

105

Pietro Staggio (1754 – before 1814). Pygmalion and Galatea. Marble. Height 235 cm. The Hermitage. Gift of King Stanislas-Augustus of Poland to Paul I

Paolo Triscorni (d. 1833). Cleopatra. Late 18th century. Marble. Height 138 cm. The Hermitage. From the Paul I collection

Paul I personally supervised the sculptural decoration of his residence, the Michael Castle. "Cleopatra" by Paolo Triscorni was placed in the central niche of the main staircase. It had to evoke in the visitor a vague understanding of the "Russian Hamlet's" tragedy and his abhorrence of his dead mother.

Antonio Canova (1757–1822). Cupid and Psyche. 1796. Marble. Height 137 cm; length 172 cm. The Hermitage. From the Empress Josephine collection, Malmaison Castle near Paris

During his career as a sculptor Antonio Canova repeatedly turned to the subject of Cupid and Psyche. The Hermitage group, with Psyche reclining, was made for Prince Yusupov. Another version, with both figures standing, was commissioned by the Empress Josephine. After her death Alexander I bought it from her son, Eugène Beauharnais.

Eduard Hau (1807 – about 1870).
The Rotunda in the Winter Palace.
Watercolour. 41.5 × 32.4 cm.
The Hermitage

Konstantin Ukhtomsky (1818–1881).
Room of the Antiquities of the
Cimmerian Bosporus. About 1853.
Watercolour. 37.8 × 30.6 cm.
The Hermitage

Luigi Premazzi (1814–1891). View of the New Hermitage from the South-east. 1861. Watercolour. 32 × 43.6 cm. The Hermitage

109

Eduard Hau (1807 – about 1870).
The Pavilion Hall in the Small
Hermitage. 1864. Watercolour.
35.1 × 41.3 cm. The Hermitage

*Boris Green. The Winter Palace
on Fire in 1837. 1838. Watercolour.
24.7 × 34.2 cm. The Hermitage*

Vasily Vereshchagin. Room in
Alexander Basilewsky's Paris
House. 1870. Watercolour.
The Hermitage

Plate with the representation of a
shepherd. 527–565. Byzantium. Silver.
Diam. 23.8 cm. The Hermitage. From
the Klimovo treasure found in 1907

From Alexander II to the End of the Romanov Dynasty

The tutorship of the future Tsar Alexander II was entrusted to the poet Vasily Zhukovsky, contact which was bound to influence the young man. Zhukovsky, no mean artist himself, sought to cultivate in the Crown Prince an interest in art and a sense of beauty. During Alexander's great European tour of 1838, his tutor made the following entry in his Diary: "To painters' studios with the Crown Prince... We visited Overbeck, Severn, Williams, Soulavie, and Ingres. We saw all the schools. Hence to Thorwaldsen's workshop, which gave a new lease of life to our failing powers."

In the same year, Zhukovsky commissioned for the Crown Prince, in the Düsseldorf studio of Theodor Hildebrandt, a painting of an idyllic subject: *Children in Anticipation of the Christmas Tree* (now in the Hermitage); from Friedrich Overbeck in Rome, his *Triumph of Religion in Art* (now in the Hermitage), and from Jean Auguste Ingres, *The Virgin Worshipping the Communion Cup* (now in the Pushkin Museum of Fine Arts, Moscow).

For all that, the tutor saw how limited were his possibilities to influence the character of the future Emperor. We find in his Diary the following sober reflections: "Since our return, the Crown Prince has been made to do the commanding from morning till night. Here we play at war and enjoy the parades of the military, and all the while, in the back country, people's throats are being cut and their houses set on fire — but no troops can be spared to go and put down the brigands."

Zhukovsky recommended his father-in-law, the Düsseldorf painter Gerhardt von Reutern, to the attention of the Crown Prince. In 1813, Reutern had lost his right arm during the Battle of the Nations near Leipzig, yet he did not give up his studies with the painter Karl Senff. Nicholas I's collection included a series of Reutern's portraits of soldiers (now in the Hermitage). In 1849, sending to St Petersburg one more canvas by his father-in-law, Zhukovsky wrote to the heir apparent: "Now my armless invalid, owing to the subsidies allotted him from above, which enabled him to form his talent at Düsseldorf, has risen to join a ranks of the first-rate painters of our day." Let us be lenient to the exaggerated opinion of a loving son-in-law... Anyhow, the work in question, sent with this letter, was given a place of honour in the New Hermitage Gallery of the Russian School, as we can see from Eduard Hau's watercolour of 1856. The Reutern canvas, *Abraham's Sacrifice* (now in the Russian Museum), was placed all too close to Rembrandt's picture of the same subject.

In Zhukovsky's educational system, the aesthetic aspect was inseparable from the ethical. It was decided that during his tour of Russia, the Crown Prince should visit Siberia as well. His talks with the exiled Decembrists doubtlessly influenced his later decision to grant them amnesty, which was proclaimed immediately on Alexander ascending the throne. The Emperor's patronage of Alexander Ivanov and Mark Antokolsky, his support of the Itinerants and the interest he took in their art were all due to Zhukovsky's formative influence on him as Crown Prince. There is a tradition that Alexander was displeased with Vereshchagin's series of anti-war pictures. It is asserted that the artist would not show him round when the Emperor and his heir visited the exhibition. Upon which, it is said, Alexander II advised the Prussian general Werder to buy Vereshchagin's battle scenes for the purpose of destroying them. But this story seems questionable, since two canvases from Vereshchagin's brush (now in the Russian Museum) were kept at Alexander II's Farm Palace in Peterhof.

The young Tsar set himself the aim of putting the Hermitage affairs in exemplary order. In the process of checking the entries in the old inventory of the picture gallery, numerous cases were revealed of unregistered transference of paintings. It appears from Franz Labensky's explanations that in the reign of Paul I paintings were often transferred from one palace to another without any written orders, merely on the Emperor's oral instructions. Also, many discrepancies were found between the lists

Gian Pietro Campana (1808–1880).
Engraving. Bibliothèque
Nationale, Paris

of objects earmarked for the 1854 sale and the marks "sold" in the inventory. Over 350 paintings were not registered at all.

In the newly compiled inventory of 1856–59, and those which followed it, paintings belonging to the Tsar's or his family's private collections were not included. Such pictures, housed in the private suites of imperial palaces, were catalogued separately. This legalized the new status of the picture gallery: while still a part of the Imperial household, it was no longer the Emperor's private collection.

In 1856, a detailed guide to the Hermitage Department of Antiquities by Ludolph Stephani was published in the miscellanea *Propylaea*.

In 1860 came a *Description of the Museum of the Imperial Hermitage,* edited by Florian Gille, Keeper of the Department of Antiquities. First published in French, it was soon followed by a Russian translation. The description dealt only with the ground floor exhibitions; the Hermitage staff were not prepared to tackle this new catalogue. Its final editing was accomplished by Gustav Waagen, Director of the picture gallery of the Berlin Museum, specially invited to St Petersburg for the purpose in 1860. An outstanding authority on Old Masters' painting and one of the scholars who placed the study of art history on a scientific basis, he laid the beginnings of the scholary investigation of the Hermitage collection. Waagen visited St Petersburg twice. His first visit resulted in the publication of a critical catalogue of the Hermitage picture gallery, with additional information on the Academy of Arts Museum and some private collections found in St Petersburg. During his second visit in 1861, Waagen compiled a Memorandum containing his suggestions for the improvement of the Museum exposition. He recommended that the pictures should not be hung too close to one another, or too high up. A band of vacant space, approximately two *arshins* in height (an *arshin* is equal to 27.95 inches) was to be left at the top of the wall. The reason for

this was, that with the system of arrangement in current use, many important pictures were hung so high above the viewer's line of vision that they could not be seen properly and were registered only in passing as part of the wall decoration. This difficulty had been realized in his time by Fiodor Bruni who suggested providing visitors with spyglasses. Some of Waagen's recommendations, such as his advice to protect the murals in the Gallery of the History of Old Painting with textile hangings, or to have pictures of the Russian School transferred to the Academy of Arts, were rejected. But the general principle was adopted, and in the winter of 1870–71 the paintings were rearranged on a new plan.

Waagen was also asked to select paintings from the Hermitage collection for transfer to the Rumiantsev Museum in Moscow, and a total of 201 were sent there (now they are in the Pushkin Museum of Fine Arts, Moscow).

An important landmark in the history of the Hermitage was the acquisition of the Campana collection in 1861. Marquis Gian Pietro Campana, Director of a Roman loan bank and an enthusiastic amateur archaeologist, had succeeded in assembling a unique collection of antiquities, partly bought, partly found during his excavations of ancient sites. His was the most representative collection of all formed around the mid-19th century and it was known all over Europe. As far back as 1851, Campana had offered his collection to the Russian government, but the negotiations led to nothing, owing to the exorbitant price demanded by the Marquis.

Meanwhile Campana went on collecting. He added to his antiquities a rich picture gallery and collections of Renaissance majolica and sculptures. Finally financial difficulties forced him to resort to illegal practices. He sent to Paris a confidential agent to arrange for the sale of some jewellery objects kept in his loan bank as securities. Interested persons called for an audit; a deficit of one million scudi was disclosed (the amount largely depended on the valuation of the securities), and the Marquis found

Stepan Gedeonov (1815–1878).
Lithographed photograph

himself in the dock. Further inquiry made it clear that not only were the Marquis's house and villa crammed with treasures of art, but that all the ready money belonging to his loan bank had been transformed into securities in the form of paintings, sculptures, and vases which filled all the storerooms. In 1858, Marquis Campana was found guilty and condemned to twenty years in the galleys. The Pope substituted lifelong exile for penal servitude. The property of the Marquis was to be sold by auction to pay off the debts. The sale to come caused a veritable diplomatic war between prospective bidders. Agents of the British Museum who offered too low a sum met with a refusal. The agent of the Louvre turned in his anxiety to Napoleon III, begging him to prevent the English from becoming the owners of these masterpieces of art, for — he argued — they were not worthy to possess them.

The papal government granted the Russian agent, Stepan Gedeonov, the privilege of preliminary choice. When this became known, a tide of protests rose in the French press. Men like Jean Ingres, Eugène Delacroix, Prosper Mérimée, and Alexandre Dumas raised their voices in defence of the unity of the collection. Campana himself, already pardoned by the Pope, published in the newspaper *Nazione* of 23 February 1861 an indignant article against the breaking down of the collection by Russian agents. But Gedeonov had already managed "to skim the cream off the collection", as newspaper reporters put it. The French Academician Louis Vitet complained in public that, in addition to the Queen of Vases ("Regina vasorum") and some 20 more vessels of the same style, the Russians appropriated 35 colossal vases from Ruvo. What he meant by the Queen of Vases, was the unique hydria from Cumae, with polychrome relief decoration. As far back as 1854, the archaeologist Desiré Raoul-Rochette had called it a marvel and declared that he knew of no other art work compared to it.

On the whole, Gedeonov succeeded in securing 500 vases, 193 bronzes, and 78 sculptures. He was aware of the true value of his acquisitions. In a letter to St Petersburg, he wrote of the relief of the *Slaughter of the Niobids*: "It is a poem in marble! Alexander II got it for 125,000 scudi, whereas Napoleon III would have had to pay 812,000!"

The Campana collection enriched the Hermitage Department of Antiquities with materials of exceeding importance. Some of its parts, such as the Etruscan monuments or Italic vases and bronzes, have undergone hardly any changes in their structure up to the present day. Others, like the antique statuary including portrait sculptures, gave a finishing touch to the Hermitage collection. The sculptures of the nine Muses, of Augustus as Jupiter enthroned, the colossal statue of Jupiter seated, which gave its name to the Jupiter Room, are the pride of the Museum. Later, a corner room in the Department of Antiquities, decorated in imitation of the courtyard of a Hellenistic house, also got its name of the Aura Room from a Campana sculpture in the centre.

The famous Queen of Vases pronounced by Raoul-Rochette to be "the crowning jewel of Campana's famous museums", came into the Marquis's possession in a rather roundabout, not to say dishonest manner. It was found at Cumae in 1853 during the excavations conducted there by Count Leopoldo of Syracuse, brother to the King of Naples. The workers kept it back for private sale after the closure of the digging.

In addition to the antiquities, Stepan Gedeonov secured some fresco paintings from Raphael's studio. Once they used to decorate the so-called Villa Spada on the Palatine Hill. Its last owners were monks who thought the subjects of the frescoes too frivolous for a monastery. In 1856, the frescoes were separated from the walls, transferred to canvas by the artist Antonio Succhi and sold to Marquis Campana. It is much to be deplored that Gedeonov, absorbed in the affair of the frescoes, should have failed to pay due attention to the rest of the Campana picture gallery — it contained 450 paintings by Italian 15th- and 16th-century artists. They were acquired by the Louvre.

117

Piotr Saburov. Engraving after a drawing by P.F. Borel

The arrival of the Campana collection necessitated the enlargement of the display area belonging to the growing Department of Antiquities. To give it extra room, the Hermitage Library was transferred to the Public Library of St Petersburg; the collections of the graphic arts, to the Gallery of the Fine Arts; and sculptures of the modern period, to the first-floor landing of the Grand Staircase in the New Hermitage. A contemporary, Dmitry Grigorovich, justly wrote that "with the advent of the enormous Campana collection, the Hermitage, at a stroke, acquired European significance".

After having so brilliantly carried off the Campana transaction, Stepan Gedeonov was appointed Director of the Hermitage. In 1863, Alexander II approved the list of the Museum's staff. This was a final step in the process of transforming the Hermitage, at long last, into a museum like all others, managed by a director. Gedeonov proved to be perfectly equal to his task. He was fully aware of the great importance of the new institution. His concept of it is formulated in the 1865 Report to the Minister of the Imperial Court, who offered to transfer some of the Hermitage duplicates to the museum at Odessa. Gedeonov wrote in answer: "All museums set the greatest value on the completeness of their collections; in this case, where the unparalleled collection of antiquities from the Cimmerian Bosporus is concerned, the Hermitage regards its integrity as a matter of vital importance, and itself ... as responsible for this integrity to the whole of Russia... It is on the perfect preservation of even the least trifles connected with such discoveries, that the very significance of the Imperial Museum depends in its quality as sole owner of unique archaeological collections of world importance." In conformity with his view of the Hermitage as a treasure-house of "the whole of Russia", Gedeonov insisted on the annulment of the requirements recorded in the admission rules. The obsolete regulations which confined the contingent of visitors to persons wearing frock-coats or uniforms had been introduced by Nicholas I. These were the first to be annuled; later, in 1866, Gedeonov carried his point concerning the abolition of admission by ticket.

The number of paintings acquired during Gedeonov's term of office was relatively small but they included two masterpieces of world renown. In 1864, Count of Litta, related to an Italian family with Russian connections and owning a family picture gallery in Milan, made an offer of some pictures to the Hermitage. Gedeonov selected four canvases and bought them for 100,000 francs. The most important among this batch was the celebrated *Madonna and Child* by Leonardo da Vinci, known to this day as the *Madonna Litta*.

In 1869, a similar offer was made to the Museum by Count Conestabile, also owner of a family picture gallery. Its chief treasure was Raphael's *Madonna and Child,* much desired by the Empress Maria Fiodorovna. In spite of the Count's first refusal to sell it at the price proposed and in spite of the protests of the Italian public, Gedeonov succeeded in acquiring the rare masterpiece. The *Madonna Conestabile* was displayed in the Hermitage as the Empress's property until 1880 when it passed to the Museum in execution of Maria Fiodorovna's bequest, together with Domenichino's *St John the Divine.*

The Hermitage now seemed to have attained the apogee of its greatness. In 1865, Grigorovich wrote that "the importance of the Hermitage for Russia is proved by the fact that, although some years ago it was accessible only to a few, and although our society does not manifest a strong leaning towards art, the Hermitage, nevertheless, enjoys an enormous popularity in our society. Just say the word, Hermitage! All over Russia, everyone has heard of it already. Even people who have never been to St Petersburg will ask questions about it". But for all that, the Hermitage had its weak points. There were no specialized exhibitions of the decorative arts; the collection of the Russian School of painting was behind the times and examples of 19th-century painting were entirely lacking.

Sergei Egornov (1860–1920). Portrait of Piotr Semionov-Tien-Shansky. 1903. Oil on canvas. 151 × 107 cm. The Russian Museum, St Petersburg

As far back as the 1830s, Nikolai Smirnov (whose wife, Alexandra Smirnova-Rosset, was a celebrated society hostess who cultivated the acquaintance of poets, artists, and authors) wrote in a letter to Vasily Zhukovsky: "How often have I regretted that our men of wealth, having the Hermitage within their reach, will not donate a hundred thousand or thereabouts to establish a gallery of paintings by artists of today. In twenty years' time such a gallery would be priceless."

In the middle of the century, the drawing-rooms of the Petersburg élite were hung with canvases by contemporary Western painters: a tribute to European fashion. Théophile Gautier left a description of a typical drawing-room of this kind in his *Voyage en Russie:* "Si le maître de la maison se pique d'être amateur, à coup sûr du damas rouge des Indes, de la brocatelle aux orfrois sombres se détacheront éclairés par de puissants réflecteurs encadrés des plus riches bordures, un Horace Vernet, un Gudin, un Calame, un Koekkoek… ou, s'il veut faire preuve de patriotisme, un Brulov et un Aïvasovsky; — ce sont les peintres les plus à la mode: notre école moderne n'est pas encore parvenue là-bas. Cependant nous avons rencontré deux ou trois Meissonier et à peu près autant de Troyon. La manière de nos peintres ne semble pas assez finie aux Russes."

At the 1851 exhibition of art objects from private collections, organized in St Petersburg by the Duke of Leuchtenberg, President of the Academy of Arts, contemporary painting was represented by the same names as those on Gautier's list, with the only addition of François Winterhalter, author of numerous portraits of St Petersburg society beauties. Of the collection of pictures by artists of the modern period, the most remarkable were those of Chancellor Alexander Gorchakov and Count Nikolai Kushelev-Bezborodko. The latter had inherited part of the enormous gallery of Alexander Bezborodko, the statesman of Catherine II's reign. In a short space of time, approximately five years, he added to it a collection of

paintings, mostly by French artists of his own day. Such collections were extremely few at the time. Still quite a young man, Count Kushelev-Bezborodko proved able to appreciate properly the art of the leading masters of the epoch. His collection included works by painters such as Théodore Rousseau, Jules Dupré, Díaz, Eugène Delacroix, Alexandre Decamps, Gustave Courbet, Jean Millet, and Constant Troyon. In those days, landscapes of the Barbizon School, which seem to us so ingenuous, so artless, peaceful, and poetic, met with utter incomprehension and provoked indignation and open hostility on the part of official critics and the majority of the bourgeois public.

In the spring of 1862, Count Kushelev-Bezborodko died at Nice. His will contained a clause by which a splendid gift was left to the Gallery of the Academy of Arts: "My pictures and statues I do bequeath to the Academy of Arts for the creation of a public gallery, to be continually open to artists and the public, accessible without any restriction as to the form of dress." The latter was an allusion to the rule still in force at the Imperial Hermitage and later annulled by Gedeonov. The Kushelev Gallery, as it was popularly known in the capital, was the only public museum of modern Western art and remained so until the post-revolutionary period. It contained 466 paintings and 29 sculptures. In 1922, the Gallery was incorporated into the Hermitage.

The Emperor Alexander III, who ascended the Russian throne in 1881, was not devoid of interest in art. In 1870, he had had the greater part of a collection of Russian paintings, assembled by Vasily Kokorev, tax-farmer and industrialist, bought for him in Moscow, and placed in the Alexander Palace at Tsarskoye Selo. As Crown Prince, Alexander, together with his wife Maria Fiodorovna — the Danish Princess Dagmar — took lessons in painting from the well-known landscapist Alexander Bogoliubov. In his *Memoirs,* Bogoliubov recalled how "at Berensdorf (Denmark) the Crown Prince started buying up ancient

119

Léon Bakst (1866–1924). Portrait of Alexander Benois. 1898. Watercolour, pastel. 64.5 × 100.3 cm. The Russian Museum, St Petersburg

silverwork, glass, and porcelain, passing imperceptibly to furniture, Gobelins tapestries, paintings". All these acquisitions formed Alexander III's private collection, housed in the Anichkov Palace where they filled several rooms. Such Hermitage canvases as Greuze's *Tête d'Amour,* or Jean Léon Gérome's *Pool in a Harem,* come from this "Museum". A number of paintings had been bought from Dmitry Grigorovich and some acquired at the Grigory Kushelev-Bezborodko sale in Paris in 1869.

In 1879, Prince Alexander Vasilchikov, who had spent his young years in the diplomatic service abroad, became Director of the Hermitage. Two years later, in 1881, he presented an official report on the state of things in the Museum. Some twenty-five years ago, he wrote, the Hermitage was well-nigh the first of the world museums. In the early 1860s it had a certain period of revival; but its further growth was retarded a few years later, due to a policy of strict economy — and that at a time when all other European museums were constantly progressing. "As soon as no steps are made forward," he concluded, "thereby a step backward is made." The new Director succeeded in obtaining financial independence from the Ministry of the Court, but it was a Pyrrhic victory. The sum that the Hermitage was able to allot for new acquisitions out of its own financial resources amounted to a miserable 5,000 roubles! That accounts for the fact that the only work of the Western schools of painting acquired abroad before the 1917 revolution was the fresco of Fra Angelico, which came to the Hermitage in 1882. This was an important purchase, made in accordance with the programme outlined in the Report a year before, which said: "Of the works by ancient Italian artists, so helpful and necessary for the study of the history and achievements of painting, we have virtually none."

With a view to the development of the Hermitage picture gallery, Vasilchikov turned his attention, first and foremost, to domestic sources, i.e. palace collections. In 1882, twenty-two canvases of the Dutch School were transferred to the Museum from Peter the Great's Palace of Monplaisir at Peterhof, where they ran a serious risk of perishing from the damp. This batch included Rembrandt's *David Parting from Jonathan*. A number of paintings came from Gatchina, with Tiepolo's *Maecenas Presenting the Liberal Arts to Augustus,* Boucher's *Pastoral Scene* and his *Landscape with a Pond* — formerly items of the Hermitage collection from which they had been removed. The Gallery of Objects de vertu was enriched by items from the Winter Palace, part of the household property. In 1883, permanent exhibitions of porcelains and silverwork from the palace stores were mounted in the Winter Palace. They formed a new section of the Museum, situated on the second floor and little accessible to the general public.

In the same years the Imperial Stables Museum was founded, containing, in addition to historic carriages, a collection of Gobelins tapestries. Common to all museums in early 19th-century Europe was a concentration on the works of the fine arts, as they were then called. Nicholas I's Arsenal was probably the only exception. Objects of the decorative arts were preserved in *Kunstkammers* or else displayed among objects de vertu. It was not until the 1830s that museums developed an interest in medieval and Renaissance artistic craftsmanship.

Systematic collecting of objects of the decorative arts began in the middle of the 19th century. It was coupled with a tendency for reviving artistic craftsmanship as a branch of industry. A Museum of Artistic Craftsmanship, sponsored by the Society for the Encouragement of the Arts, was founded in 1870 by Dmitry Grigorovich; and a Museum attached to the Alexander Stieglitz School of Industrial Design, by Alexander Polovtsov in 1884. After 1917, both museums joined the Hermitage.

His first acquisition of articles of artistic craftsmanship was made by Prince Vasilchikov in 1884, when he bought the Piotr Saburov collection. Its owner, former Ambassador to Greece, amassed a collection of rare antiquities dur-

Portrait of Alexander Polovtsov.
Photograph after an engraving. 1881

ing his sojourn in that country. In 1880, he was appointed Ambassador to Berlin, whence he was recalled in 1884. He sold his marbles to the Berlin Museum, his painted vases and bronzes to the British Museum; but the most valuable part of his collection he offered to the Hermitage. This was a complex of terracotta statuettes, acquired from treasure hunters during the unlicensed diggings in the necropolis of ancient Tanagra in the 1870s. In February 1884, Saburov wrote to Polovtsov, then Secretary of State: "I have reserved the most valuable part, the terracottas; in my negotiation with London and Berlin, I stipulated that here preference should be given to the Hermitage." Again, as in the case of the Campana collection, political passions rose to fever pitch. After a talk with Polovtsov, Ivan Vorontsov-Dashkov, Minister of the Court, addressed the Director of the Hermitage in the following words: "All the great museums of Europe have now focused their attention on this collection. We have a dangerous rival in the Berlin Museum. Our young Kieseritzky saw the collection in Athens and in Berlin and says that each object in it is worth its weight in gold. God forbid lest its acquisition should add fresh lustre to the Berlin Museum, so rich already!" Soon, in April of the same year, 233 Tanagra statuettes arrived in St Petersburg. Polovtsov made in his Diary the following entry, with a tangible sense of satisfaction: "Going to see the clay figurines [Tanagra] of the Saburov collection, displayed at the Hermitage. Very glad to have had a share in preventing a loss of these objects to Russia, poor as it is in examples of artistic craftsmanship." Some time later the 'Tanagrettes' were shown to the public. Saburov proved perfectly right in his conjecture, worded in a letter to Vasilchikov, that "in the coming winter they shall be the stars of the Petersburg season. Your Kerch Room with my Tanagras will surpass in this respect all the museums of the world". In 1886, Valentin Serov wrote: "During my last trip to Peter (short for St Petersburg. — *Tr.'s note*) I was at the Hermitage. It has been a long time since I have had such a feeling of lively beauty as that aroused in me by the tiny Greek figurines, almost toys; but these toys are perhaps worth a good half of the cold Roman sculptures." Serov invented a special term, Tanagretics, to apply to works of art showing sincerity and spontaneous inspiration.

At the same period another purchase was made of considerable importance to the structure of the Hermitage collections. That was the collection of the Russian diplomat Alexander Basilewsky, residing in Paris. It took him forty years in the making, and consisted of objects of applied and decorative arts from the medieval and Renaissance epochs; in assembling them, Basilewsky hoped to represent eventually a full history of Christian art from the 1st to the 16th centuries. During his visit to Paris as Crown Prince, Alexander III saw the collection, which created a sensation at the 1878 World Exhibition. Alexander's Secretary of State, Polovtsov, himself a collector of note, exerted his influence in favour of the purchase. The entry in his Diary, dated 21 January 1884, says: "Suggested to Vorontsov that we should not stop at the acquisition of the Saburov collection; that the Basilewsky collection in Paris should also be bought and placed — with the addition of the best objects from the Arsenal at Tsarskoye Selo — in the spacious and well-lighted rooms where the cases with medals now stand." The painter Bogoliubov, who used to teach painting to Alexander, also did his best to influence his former pupil. The sale, planned for the spring of 1885, was anxiously expected in Paris; connoisseurs predicted that it would far surpass the celebrated 1860 sale of the Saltykov collection with its record profit of almost two million francs. On 11 November 1884, Polovtsov wrote in his Diary: "The Emperor's consent to the purchase of the Basilewsky collection. Telegraphed to Bogoliubov, 'Consider affair decided in principle'. The purchase to be made out of the Emperor's private purse."

On the morning following the deal, the Parisian world of antiquaries and connoisseurs was shocked by the publications in the press, from which they learned that the

Emile Auguste Charles Carolus-Duranc (1838–1917). Portrait of Nadezhda Polovtsova. 1876. Oil on canvas. 206.5 × 124.5 cm. The Hermitage. From the Alexander Polovtsov collection

expected sale, the hit of the season, was not to take place, the Basilewsky collection having been sold on the previous evening to the Russian government for a sum of six million francs, — and that "on the strength of an ordinary telegram!" Even President Grévy himself, who had never before manifested the slightest interest in art, thought it his duty to go and see the collection before its shipment to St Petersburg.

On its arrival the collection was arranged in the New Hermitage Rooms of Coins and Medals and shown to Alexander III. Polovtsov made a triumphant entry in his Diary: "I cannot stop exulting about having had a hand in its acquisition. No objects of this kind are to be found in Russia, and hitherto they were accessible only to those of my compatriots who had the means to travel; now the sight of them is available to the meanest workman. The Emperor is interested in every item in the collection and thanks me again and again for my part in its purchase."

The new accessions, greatly increasing the Museum's holdings, served as a basis for the formation of the Department of Medieval and Renaissance Art. The Department, founded in 1885, incorporated the arms and armour from the Arsenal at Tsarskoye Selo. Premises for it were assigned on the ground floor of the New Hermitage, formerly occupied by the Council of State which had moved to the Maria Palace. In 1866, whilst still in the process of formation, the Department was complemented by the Golitsyn Museum acquired in Moscow; it was based on collections assembled by 18th-century connoisseurs.

The new Department was opened to the public in 1888. It placed the Hermitage on the same footing as the Louvre and the Musée de Cluny in Paris and the Victoria and Albert Museum in London. The purchase of the Basilewsky collection must be regarded as one of the most happy, even epoch-making episodes in the history of the Hermitage. It included examples of Early Christian and Byzantine art, ancient ecclesiastic objects in the Roman-

esque and Gothic styles, ivory carvings, enamels, majolica, glassware, and faience.

The Department of Medieval and Renaissance Art was headed by the eminent Russian scholar Nikodim Kondakov. His Memorandum, dealing with the work of the Museum's new section, outlines the problems which face it and which several generations of scholars and art collectors have been working to solve since his day. This is what he wrote about the cardinal problem of the Department: "To establish the links between Russian antiquities and the Orient is the most important task of Russian science and of our archaeological collection." In 1889, Kondakov's assistant Vladimir Bock gave to the Hermitage his collection of Coptic fabrics, assembled during his expedition to Egypt. Yakov Smirnov, who succeeded Kondakov in 1898, laid the beginnings of scholastic research in Oriental silverwork.

In comparison with the bustling activity prevailing in the new department, or with the unceasing stream of antiquities pouring in from the Imperial Archaeological Commission, the development of the Picture Gallery seemed to have come to a halt. The sum of 5,000 roubles allotted annually out of the Museum's budget for the purchase of paintings was far too small for acquisitions on a scale at all comparable with those of Catherine II or Nicholas I. But with the acquisition of the Golitsyn collection the Hermitage received two works of the greatest importance: a triptych by Perugino (now in the National Gallery of Art, Washington), and *The Annunciation* by Cima da Conegliano (now in the Hermitage). Also, Prince Vasilchikov made two splendid acquisitions in Russia itself: the missing half of Rogier van der Weyden's *St Luke Drawing a Portrait of the Virgin*, and the reverse of the wings from Lucas van Leyden's triptych *The Healing of the Blind Man of Jericho*, sold in 1854 and now recovered from the St Petersburg antiquary Aaron Kaufmann.

The reign of Nicholas II was marked in the Hermitage by the closing down of exhibitions of Russian paintings.

Yamachita Rin (1857-1939). Icon: The Resurrection (obverse and reverse). About 1891. Japan. Papier-mâché, oil, varnish. 32 × 26.5 cm. The Hermitage. Gift to Crown Prince Nicholas, 1891

The works of the Russian School were transferred to the Russian Museum of the Emperor Alexander III, opened in 1898 in the Michael Palace, St Petersburg. The former premises of the Russian School were used for the display of French paintings transferred from Velten's Old Hermitage.

The newly formed Russian Museum received into its possession, apart from the paintings from the Hermitage and the Winter Palace, materials from other sources, such as the Academy of Arts, the Alexander Palace at Tsarskoye Selo, and the collection of Prince Lobanov-Rostovsky, bought by Nicholas II. The young Tsar himself donated to the Museum, out of his private collection, over forty canvases by Russian artists, such as Vasily Vereshchagin, Apollinary Vasnetsov, Vasily Perov, Ivan Shishkin, and Vladimir Makovsky.

The new Tsar's collecting was not to be compared with that of his predecessors. Yet he must be allowed a certain interest in art. It is known that Nicholas II, together with Savva Mamontov and Maria Tenisheva, subsidized and supported the journal *Mir Iskusstva (The World of Art)*, and by doing so helped the Society of that name. True, this was done at the request of Valentin Serov, then engaged in painting the Emperor's portrait. Taking offence at some of the Empress's critical remarks, Serov dropped the work, leaving the portrait unfinished; to Sergei Diaghilev, his friend and fellow member of the World of Art Society, who attempted to put things right he telegraphed the following stinging reply from Moscow: "I will no longer serve in this house!" During the First Russian Revolution of 1905, Serov satirized the person of Nicholas II and denounced his politics in biting cartoons. One of his bitterly mocking drawings, the famous *Soldiers, Soldiers, Heroes Every One, Is This Your Glory?*, he presented to Maxim Gorky.

The repertory of paintings chosen by Nicholas II for his private collection reveals his trivial taste. With the sole exception of Vasily Surikov's monumental *Ermak's Conquest of Siberia* (now in the Russian Museum), they are mostly works by mediocre painters of inferior talent, such as Alexander Kiseliov, Nikolai Bogdanov, Konstantin Makovsky, Mikhail Khlodovsky, or Pavel Briullov. The same is true of the canvases of French artists bought by the Emperor in 1896 at the exhibition of French art in St Petersburg. Jules Lefévre's *Mary Magdalene in a Grotto* and François Flameng's series of five pictures with scenes from the life of Napoleon are typical examples of "salon" art and had enormous success with the undiscriminating public. Lefévre's painting is of some interest only inasmuch as it used to be owned by Alexandre Dumas the Young before it came into the possession of the Tsar of Russia.

The fresh breath of the First Revolution gradually began to infiltrate the stuffy atmosphere of the Imperial Museum with its unshakeable rules, apparently impervious to change. Thus, after 1905, court festivities and supper parties were no longer held in the rooms of the Hermitage: it was felt to be inappropriate. Questions were asked in the Third Duma about this. Deputy Piotr Surkov, a weaver from Kostroma, speaking on behalf of the Social Democratic group, declared: "We want no museums or galleries closed to the people. The halls hung with masterpieces by great artists are used by pages, *Kammerherrs,* and maids-of-honour to dance in and have supper parties. I think it to be sacrilegious in respect of the great works and their authors." The journalist Sergei Makovsky gave to his article on the Hermitage the mortifying title of *Sepulchre of Art* (1907). This is what he wrote: "A truly dead silence reigns in our museum halls. All is mould-grown. For years things are not moved, stay where they used to be. For years whole departments have no additions made to them. The annual sum assigned for acquisitions to all the departments taken together comes to the perfectly absurd figure of 5,000 roubles, and no one moves a finger to change this state of things. And that is natural: the fewer changes, the less noise; the less of life the better. The 'authorities' are quite content with themselves as it is.

They could do even without visitors to the Hermitage. Why let them into the sanctum? The silence of the tomb should not be disturbed by the uninitiated."

The strenuous activity of the World of Art Society and the rapid advance of museum work in the West were sure to produce a stimulating influence on the Hermitage. Eminent scholars like Ernest Liphart, James Schmidt, and later Alexander Benois, joined the staff of the Museum's picture gallery. Whereas, on the one hand, not a few national collections, including those of Polovtsov, Delaroff, and Schlichting, were sold abroad, on the other, the country's patriotically-minded patrons of art made magnificent, absolutely priceless gifts to the Hermitage.

In 1910, the famous geographer and explorer Piotr Semionov-Tien-Shansky offered the Museum his collection, assembled over the course of fifty years and containing over 700 canvases by Dutch and Flemish masters. The Museum acquired this collection for half the price offered to the owner by foreign art dealers. The Semionov collection was to remain in his possession for the term of his natural life. It was brought to the Hermitage in 1915 for a temporary exhibition and incorporated in the Museum only after the 1917 revolution. As a study collection for research in the history of the Dutch School it was of the greatest significance to scholars. Particularly valuable were the works by the precursors of Rembrandt and those of painters of his immediate environment: Nicolaes Maes, Barnet Fabritius, and Govert Flinck.

At an exhibition mounted in 1908 by the journal *The World of Art*, Ernest Liphart identified the *Madonna Benois* as an early picture by Leonardo. His sensational discovery was immediately recognized by the experts. But when in 1912 the owners finally made up their minds to part with the painting, selling it to the Hermitage for a much lower sum than that offered them by Western antiquaries, reactionaries within the country whipped up an anti-Semitic campaign and even tried to question the

desirability of the purchase. Nevertheless, in 1914 the *Madonna Benois* entered the Museum. Another important acquisition was Perugino's *St Sebastian*, which once used to belong to Zinaida Volkonskaya. Such rare and valuable canvases as Tiepolo's *The Rape of the Sabines* (from the Campanari collection) and El Greco's *St Peter and St Paul* (from the Durnovo collection) also came to the Hermitage as gifts, largely through the efforts of Liphart.

In 1911–12, the Hermitage received by bequest several priceless works by Old Italian Masters from the hereditary collection of the Stroganovs. A reliquary of Fra Angelico and Simone Martini's *Madonna of the Annunciation* came from Grigory Stroganov's Roman collection, together with several rare examples of Sassanian silver. Pavel Stroganov, Grigory's brother, who died in St Petersburg in 1912, left to the Museum his paintings by Cima da Conegliano, Filippino Lippi, Domenichino, and Francesco Maineri.

A series of English 18th-century portraits came to the Hermitage by the bequest of Alexei Khitrovo in 1912. It included the best of the Museum's specimens of English portraiture: the works of Thomas Gainsborough, George Romney, Thomas Lawrence, and Henry Raeburn.

This short period of revival, marked by the activities of private collectors who entered into collaboration with the Museum, came to an abrupt end with the outbreak of World War I and the February revolution of 1917. Valuable art works were packed in all haste and sent to Moscow. In 1914, only the Gallery of Objects de vertu had been evacuated. In 1917, the Provisional Government decreed that the collections of the "former Imperial Hermitage" should be despatched to Moscow, together with the property of the Imperial Household belonging to the Winter Palace. The evacuated museum treasures were deposited in the Kremlin and the building of the History Museum on Red Square.

Vase from Cumae ("Regina vasorum").
4th century B.C. Italy.
Height 56 cm. The Hermitage.
From the Campana collection

On account of its beauty of form and
decoration this black-lacquered hydria,
initially adorned with a polychrome relief,
was called the Queen of Vases — "Regina
vasorum". As far back as 1854, one
of the leading archaeologists of the time,
Raoul-Rochette, declared that he knew
no other art work comparable to it.

Cinerary urn: A Reclining Youth.
4th century B.C. Etruria. Bronze.
Height 42 cm. The Hermitage.
From the Campana collection

This bronze cinerary urn, "A Reclining
Youth", was unearthed in 1842 in an
Etruscan necropolis in the vicinity of
Perugia. While in the Campana collection, it was known as "An Etruscan
Nobleman". When the collection was
divided between various museums, the
gold ornaments originally kept inside
the urn found their way to the Louvre.

Spinner and Cupid. 3rd century B.C.
Tanagra. Terracotta. Height 18.5 cm.
The Hermitage. From the Piotr
Saburov collection

One of the most valuable collections of
terracotta statuettes from the Tanagra
necropolis was assembled by Piotr
Saburov, Russian Ambassador to Greece.
When these remarkable clay figurines
were displayed in European museums
and at the Paris World Exhibition, they
caused a real sensation. "Spinner and
Cupid" is one of the most beautiful
items in the Hermitage collection.

126

*Unknown 15th-century Nether-
landish artist. St Michael. Wood.
Height 128 cm. The Hermitage. From
the Alexander Basilewsky collection*

*St Michael is represented trampling the
dragon, a personification of evil and sin.
A watercolour by Vereshchagin shows a
room in Basilewsky's Paris house where
this sculpture occupied a place of honour.*

*Diptych with circus scenes.
6th century. Byzantium. Ivory.
33 × 10.5 cm. The Hermitage. From
the Alexander Basilewsky collection*

*The great artistic legacy of Byzantium
is represented in the Hermitage by one
of the world's finest collections of silver,
ivory and icons.*

128

*Casket. 11th century. South Italy.
Ivory. 36.6 × 18 × 16 cm. The Her-
mitage. From the Alexander
Basilewsky collection*

*Similar caskets, together with oliphants,
ancient hunters' horns made of ivory,
were widely produced around the
Mediterranean in the 11th and 12th
centuries.*

129

Lamp. Mid-14th century. Egypt.
Glass. Height 36.2 cm; diam. 26.2 cm.
The Hermitage. From the Alexander
Basilewsky collection

The main decorative feature of this lamp
is an inscription in Arabic with a sul-
tan's name. The lamp's neck and bottom
bear heraldic emblems.

Vase with scenes from a game of polo.
13th century. Iran. Faience, painted
with lustre. Height 80 cm.
The Hermitage. From the Alexander
Basilewsky collection

The game of polo, known in Europe since
the early Middle Ages, originated in the
East where it used to be a favourite
pastime of Iranian and Caucasian
noblemen. This 13th-century lustre vase
presents figures of musicians and several
vivid scenes from a game of polo.

Bunch of Cornflowers. By Carl
Fabergé (1846–1920). Gems, enamel.
Height 19 cm. The Hermitage

Carl Fabergé, a Russian jeweller and
goldsmith, was head of a jewellery firm
which gained an international reputa-
tion. The firm specialized in new types
of objets d'art such as Easter eggs or
miniature figures of animals carved in
hardstone, though its masters continued
to produce traditional items as well —
for instance, bouquets sparkling with
precious stones.

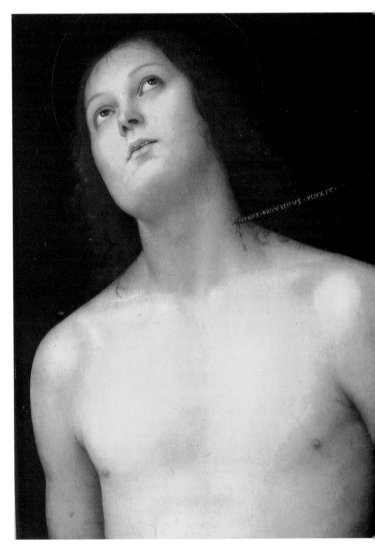

Simone Martini (about 1284 – 1344).
Madonna of the Annunciation.
Tempera on panel. 30.5 × 21.5 cm.
The Hermitage. From the Grigory
Stroganov collection, Rome

Perugino (about 1450 – 1523).
St Sebastian. About 1495. Oil and
tempera on panel. 53.5 × 39.5 cm.
The Hermitage. From the Marquise
Campanari collection, Rome (previously in the Zinaida Volkonskaya
collection)

132

Leonardo da Vinci (1452–1519). Madonna with a Flower (The Benois Madonna). Begun 1478. Oil on canvas. 49.5 × 31.5 cm. The Hermitage. From the Benois collection, Petrograd

Raphael (1483–1520). The Madonna Conestabile. Late 1502 – early 1503. Tempera on canvas. 17.5 × 18 cm. The Hermitage. From the Empress Maria Alexandrovna collection

Leonardo da Vinci (1452–1519). Madonna and Child (The Litta Madonna). 1470–90. Tempera on canvas. 42 × 43 cm. The Hermitage. From the Count of Litta collection, Milan

El Greco (1541–1614). St Peter and St Paul. Between 1587 and 1592. Oil on canvas. 121.5 × 105 cm. The Hermitage. From the Durnovo collection

Giovanni Battista Tiepolo (1696–1770). The Triumph of the Emperor. Oil on canvas. 546 × 322 cm. The Hermitage. From the Alexander Polovtsov collection

136

Thomas Gainsborough (1727–1788).
Lady in Blue. Late 1770s. Oil on
canvas. 76 × 64 cm. The Hermitage.
From the Alexei Khitrovo collection

Jean-Honoré Fragonard (1732–1806).
The Stolen Kiss. Oil on canvas.
45 × 55 cm. The Hermitage.
From the collection of King Stanislas-
Augustus of Poland

François Flameng (1856–1923).
Reception at Malmaison in 1802.
Oil on panel. 106 × 139 cm.
The Hermitage. From the Nicholas II
collection

*Jules Dupré (1811–1889). Autumn
Landscape. Oil on canvas. 51 × 46 cm.
The Hermitage. From the Nikolai
Kushelev-Bezborodko collection*

142

*Eugène Delacroix (1798–1863).
Lion Hunt in Morocco. 1854. Oil on
canvas. 74 × 92 cm. The Hermitage.
From the Nikolai Kushelev-
Bezborodko collection*

*Jean Léon Gérôme (1824–1904).
Pool in a Harem. Oil on canvas.
73.5 × 62 cm. The Hermitage.
From the Alexander III collection*

*Jules Lefebvre (1836–1912). Mary
Magdalene in a Grotto. 1876. Oil on
canvas. 71.5 × 113.5 cm. The Hermitage. From the Nicholas II collection*

*Théodore Rousseau (1812–1867).
Market in Normandy. 1830s. Oil on
panel. 29.5 × 38 cm. The Hermitage.
From the Nikolai Kushelev-
Bezborodko collection*

145

Carpet: Dog Hunt. 1889. Kyoto. Kawashima Manufactory. Silk, paper, gold thread. 440 × 290 cm. The Hermitage. Gift of the Emperor of Japan to Crown Prince Nicholas, 1891

Apart from the works of Japanese art acquired in the late 19th century, the Hermitage possesses several items brought by Crown Prince Nicholas (afterwards Nicholas II) after his visit to Japan in 1891. Nicholas bought there a great variety of art objects, though not

all of them of great artistic value. There were, however, some truly remarkable pieces. One of these was a gorgeous carpet, a masterpiece of the celebrated Kyoto weaver Kawashima Jimbei (1853–1910), who studied in Paris and mastered the technique of tapestry weaving. In 1890, the carpet was displayed at the Exhibition for the Encouragement of

National Industry. The Emperor of Japan who visited the exhibition, chose Jimbei's work as a gift to the Crown Prince Nicholas of Russia, who was expected in Japan in the near future. At that time the carpet lacked the ornamental border incorporating motifs of Japanese and Russian state arms: chrysanthemums and double-headed

eagles. It was added later by the Emperor's order. There is another story connected with the carpet. According to it, the carpet was presented to Nicholas at the close of his visit, probably by way of apology for an attempt on his life in the town of Otsu.

Interior in Ivan Morozov's mansion. Photograph. The Pushkin Museum of Fine Arts, Moscow

Vase. 1828. By Denis Joseph Marot (d. 1830). Russia. Porcelain. Height 222 cm. The Hermitage. From the Nicholas I collection

This impressive vase, presented to Nicholas I as a new-year's gift in 1829, was placed in the Round Hall of the Hermitage. One side of the vase shows a portrait of Alexander I, a map of Russia and war trophies; the other, winged female figures carrying a green sphere with a map, the word "Russia" written across it.

The Hermitage during the Soviet Period

The history of the Hermitage in the post-revolutionary period is a subject of absorbing interest and offers to the observer much food for thought. Two simultaneous but opposing processes were at work in it: the growth of the Museum's holdings and the "despoiling" of its collections. It was precisely during this period that the Hermitage grew into one of the world's greatest museums; and it was just then that it lost many of its best masterpieces and even entire collections. The accession of new materials and the formation of new departments went hand-in-hand with determined struggle for the return of Hermitage property previously removed to Moscow, and for the prevention of further withdrawals and sales.

In September 1917, the Provisional Government, alarmed at the imminent threat of public upheavals, had some of the Museum collections evacuated to Moscow. Thus, at the moment of the revolutionary outbreak the holdings of the Hermitage were already incomplete. During the events of October 1917, which came to a head in the storming of the Winter Palace, the Hermitage staff succeeded in preserving the collections — largely due to the efforts of sensible people in both the warring camps. When the Bolsheviks seized power, the Museum's administration refused to collaborate with them. Nevertheless, certain measures were taken for ensuring the safety of the collections and return of the evacuated treasures. The Hermitage also began to admit, for safe keeping, art objects from some of the private collections whose owners were leaving Petrograd* in hopes of a speedy return.

In due course, when the Museum more or less returned to normal and started to operate under the control of the new authorities, work for the preservation of

the country's artistic heritage was continued, many of the Bolshevist leaders acting to concert with the Hermitage staff.

The retrieval of the evacuated property from Moscow, where it was kept in the Kremlin, proved to be a matter of greater difficulty than could be expected. With the removal of the government to Moscow, that city resumed its historical status of the capital of Russia — now a Soviet state. Many of the newly risen cultural figures claimed that national art treasures should be concentrated there. It took an immense amount of strenuous effort, unswerving persistence, cunning policy, support of great people like the writer Maxim Gorky, and a special decree of the Soviet of People's Commissars, to bring the Hermitage collections back to Petrograd, where they were gradually prepared for display. But this happened only in 1920.

In the meanwhile, the process of nationalization of art works formerly owned by members of tsarist Russia's ruling class — now stripped by the revolution of all their property — was in full swing. Large numbers of nationalized art treasures were turned over to the Hermitage. The first accession came from other Imperial palaces: the Marble and Anichkov in Petrograd, and the Gatchina, Peterhof, and Tsarskoye Selo in its environs. It should be noted that, as a matter of fact, exchange of art objects, more especially paintings, between the Hermitage and those other residences used to be normal practice long before the revolution. In 1917, the Winter Palace adjoined by the Hermitage was declared to be "a state-owned museum on equal terms with the Hermitage". Eventually, after an attempt to turn it into a Palace of the Arts and mount there a show dedicated to revolutionary history, it gradually became a part of the Hermitage, and was used for the arrangement of its new expositions.

The art collections housed in famous palaces of Petersburg aristocracy, the Yusupovs, Stroganovs, and

---

* St Petersburg, called so after Peter the Great's patron saint, the Apostle Peter, was renamed Petrograd in 1914 and Leningrad after the death of Lenin in 1924. The original name of the city was restored in 1992.

Sheremetevs, were at first suffered to remain where they were, the palaces themselves being turned into museums; some of them, like the Stroganov palace, were even granted the status of "a branch of the Hermitage". Soon, however, their art treasures were transferred to other museums, including the Hermitage, while the premises were turned over to various governmental offices. Other private collections, most of them already incomplete, also entered the Hermitage — mainly through the State Museum Fund, a body created for the accumulation and distribution of art works.

New accessions also came from a variety of institutes, societies, commissions, and small museums, e.g. the Society for the Encouragement of the Arts, the Archaeological Society, the Russian Archaeological Institute at Constantinople. One of the most remarkable of these was a collection of Nikolai Likhachov, a Russian scholar of note. He assembled Byzantine and post-Byzantine icons, coins, and ancient written documents, including relics of great Oriental cultures of ancient past: papyri from Egypt, tables with cuneiform texts from Mesopotamia. His priceless collection, perfectly unique of its kind, originally formed a museum attached to the Institute of Books, Documents, and [the Art of] Writing, and was afterwards transferred to the Hermitage.

The accession of the collection of Count Alexei Bobrinsky, Chairman of the Archaeological Society, was an important landmark in the history of the Hermitage. Transferred from the Archaeological Society, it contained medieval Islamic bronzes, mostly from Daghestan — works generally recognized as masterpieces of the art of metalwork.

In 1922, the Hermitage received — also by transfer — the so-called Kushelev Gallery, a splendid collection of Western European paintings with a particularly rich section of 19th-century works. Assembled by several generations of the Bezborodko family, it had been willed by Nikolai Kushelev-Bezborodko to the Academy of Arts, where it entered in 1862. Also from the Academy came a beautiful collection of the Italian terracotta models and sketches for sculptural works, once part of the Farsetti collection.

The important collection of Oriental and European works of the decorative arts, belonging to the museum of the Stieglitz School of Industrial Design, entered the Hermitage, as it were, in instalments. Some collections preserved at the Russian Museum but foreign to its nature — like that of archaeological materials brought back by Piotr Kozlov from the Dead City of Khara-Khoto — were transferred to the Hermitage. In their turn, some works of Russian art went from the Hermitage to the Russian Museum. Collections of paintings and sculptures from Sinkiang, assembled by Russian expeditions to the region, came to the Hermitage from the Museum of Anthropology and Ethnography. A huge numismatic collection of Oriental provenance was received from the Academy of Sciences' Asia Museum.

The growth of the Hermitage collections and the enormous widening of their thematic range created a basis for the Museum's development into a world-important treasury of culture.

The new revolutionary powers expected from the Hermitage as sweeping ideological changes as were being carried out all over the country. The Museum was obliged to make concessions. One of the changes forced upon it was the interpretation of art phenomena in terms of vulgar sociology. That meant rearranging the expositions in such a way as to suggest to the viewer the existence of direct links between the production of art works and the process of class struggle. Many of the signs, labels, and posters were ridiculous even to the public of those days. But for all that, they served a good purpose as an excuse for

Martiros Saryan (1880–1972).
Portrait of Academician Iosif Orbeli.
Oil on canvas. 73 × 64.5 cm.
Erevan Picture Gallery

showing art works "alien to proletarian class consciousness", and thus affording to the Hermitage an opportunity to carry on its high aim of disseminating culture.

All the while, the principal changes in museum work, allegedly intended as an answer to the requirements of the epoch, were effected in such a way as, on the one hand, to avoid provoking the authorities too far, and on the other, to attain the ends really necessary for the Museum and for the country. The Hermitage was being restructured into a museum of world culture. New departments were forming. Outstanding among them was the Oriental Department, headed by the unquenchable Iosif Orbeli, subsequently Director of the Hermitage. He shaped the work of his Department so efficiently that soon it developed into a world-important centre of Oriental studies. Here were concentrated numerous cultural relics, arranged in a way to present them as phenomena of world culture, yet having an independent value of their own.

In 1931, the Department of Primitive Cultures was created for the preservation and display of most ancient materials. It grew into a centre of active archaeological exploration and research. On the eve of World War II, the Department of Russian Culture was founded; it brought together and systematized a number of enormously rich collections, including all the still available materials once associated with the Winter Palace.

The growth of old departments and the creation of the new ones had a stimulating influence on every branch of Hermitage collecting. This was largely due to the indefatigable activity and incomparable energy of its director, Iosif Orbeli. Hermitage experts conducted extensive research in different parts of the former Russian Empire. Their work combined archaeological and historical studies with collecting ob-

jects of museum value, the training of specialists, and foundation of local interest museums, especially in the former eastern governments of the Empire. They sought to reconstruct the forgotten or despised and underrated cultural history of many a nation; to place it in a proper context *vis-à-vis* world culture; and to assert the artistic merits of local cultural remains by placing them among the universally recognized masterpieces of the Hermitage collections. In the period between the 1920s and '40s, objects of archaeological and artistic interest from peripheral regions could be preserved, studied, duly appreciated, and restored only under the exceptionally favourable conditions of a central museum, like the Hermitage, supplied with necessary materials and having a properly trained staff. There it was that numerous historical and artistic relics were saved from decay and oblivion and given a worthy place in the legacy of world culture.

So large numbers of objects recovered by excavations, as well as chance finds, were brought to the Hermitage from different parts of the country, on the initiative of the Museum or that of local intelligentsia or archaeologists. Now and again, governments of the Union Republics presented to the Hermitage objects of high cultural value in gratitude for the Museum's work in their territories and to encourage the practice of Hermitage scholars in training representatives of ethnic cultures in museum specialities. This policy brought to the Museum not a few important items of archaeological, artistic, and historical value, such, for instance, as beautiful architectural details from the cities and villages of Western Central Asia; wonderful bronzes and stone reliefs from the Caucasus or a fragment of rock with an inscription cut at Tamerlane's (Timur's) command during his last campaign against the Golden Horde when he inflicted on his enemies the final crushing defeat. With the formation,

153

in different parts of the country, of local museums with their own conservation and restoration workshops, the influx of materials from the periphery ceased. One of the important aims of the Museum's cultural work was thus gained, and it could concentrate on its role as a world centre for comparative study and display of materials of the great cultures of the past.

Particularly noteworthy were the efforts made by the Hermitage, in common with other museums, in the case of salvation of works of Russian ecclesiastic art. In the 1920s, when Bolshevist authorities confiscated church property, most art treasures were melted down or else sold. It was a matter of the utmost difficulty to get these objects placed in museums as works of cultural, rather than religious significance. Characteristic of the time was the episode of saving the silverwork décor from the tomb of St Alexander Nevsky. Some prominent Russian scholars, acting at no small risk to themselves, managed to obtain a permission for the transfer to the Hermitage of this masterpiece which had been marked for melting down in a scheme of solving the state's financial problems. Great credit must also go to the Hermitage expeditions of postwar years, especially those that went to the Russian North, for they salvaged and restored large numbers of neglected and forgotten icons in a state verging on utter ruin.

Unfortunately, alongside the processes tending towards further growth and development of the Hermitage, other tendencies were at work which threatened the holdings of the Museum with serious losses. The danger came from without and took different forms. The new political reality created many possibilities for basic alterations, some of which were aimed at reducing the status of St Petersburg–Petrograd, anathematized as a symbol of tsarist autocracy. Moscow resumed its long-lost position as the capital of the country and thought itself entitled as such to deserve a Hermitage of its own. The choice fell on the Alexander III Museum of Fine Arts, created by Ivan Tsvetayev. Its transformation was to be achieved at the expense of the Hermitage — that "symbol of the hateful past" — even though there was no pressing necessity for this. And yet it was done.

The state policy of preserving the Empire under the guise of a union of socialist republics required some playing up to the peripheral regions, "bribing" them, as it were, by demonstrative acts of "atonement" for the "guilt" of the centre and of Russia as a country. The Hermitage with its wealth of extensive, well systematized collections, in its capacity of a symbol of the overthrown "exploiter state of the past", naturally suggested itself as a source to be drawn upon for the distribution of art works to different museums less richly endowed. Beginning with the year 1932, hundreds of paintings and objects of the decorative arts were transferred to picture galleries and museums all over Russia, the Ukraine, Byelorussia, the Caucasus, and other parts of the Union. Especially great was the loss of museum items to the Ukraine. Here matters of transfer were managed by a special commission which claimed to represent not individual museums, but the entire Republic. Listed in the Acts of Transfer preserved at the Hermitage registrar's office are tens of thousands of items: archaeological finds, gold- and silverwork, paintings, Zaporozhian Cossack banners, documents, objects associated with the Ukraine and not associated with it. Most of these things disappeared during World War II and are not likely ever to be recovered.

Another category of losses sustained by the Hermitage came in consequence of the young Soviet Russia's military defeats. According to the peace treaty concluded with Poland, large numbers of items of Polish provenance were restored to that country, in-

Felix Yusupov. Photograph. 1914

cluding some splendid collections of fine arms. Transfers of art works were effected in accordance with other government agreements containing clauses of a similar nature.

However disastrous for the Hermitage, these transfers were made with at least a show of political justice. None of this was in evidence in the next blow struck at the Museum by the government. By this we mean the notorious sales of objects from the Hermitage collections. The Museum was again used as a source of funds to be raised for financing the state's foreign policy and the spread of its political influence. Art works were withdrawn from the Hermitage by the thousand and sent to Europe to be auctioned off. Some of them came back: the world art market demanded masterpieces, not works of the second or even third rank. But the worst category of sales, and ones that were the most destructive to the Museum, were those that were personal-oriented, with objects passing by choice into the hands of well-known art collectors like Calouste Gulbenkian or Andrew Mellon. Such sales were aimed at ensuring certain political adventures or as compensation for services rendered. Thus, Gulbenkian arranged for the sale of Russian oil in Europe.

These buyers knew exactly what they wanted, and were in a position to insist on their demands. No less than fifty masterpieces of the first rank were sold from the Hermitage collection virtually for a song. They included Perugino's triptych of the *Crucifixion*, once owned by Golitsyn; Boticelli's *Adoration of the Magi*; two Raphaels, a Titian, a Veronese. The Hermitage lost Van Eyck's *Annunciation*, six Rembrandts, four portraits by Van Dyck and two by Hals.

It is a marvel that after all these tremendous losses the Hermitage picture gallery still remains one of the world's best.

As early as the 1920s, an Expert Commission was created for the selection and assessment of the objects of artistic interest for the purpose of increasing foreign currency fund of the Central Bank by sales of museum items and valuables from the state treasury. The sales were organized more or less secretly, all the relevant decisions being made by the People's Commissariat for Education, which served as a screen for the government. The Hermitage was powerless to prevent them by direct action. But we know that most of the Hermitage staff, in defiance of the situation where disobedience to any command motivated by the magic formula "the country needs foreign currency" (a thesis still as much in force now as ever), might mean imprisonment in a concentration camp or even a death sentence, did everything they possibly could to obstruct the selection and withdrawal of art works. There are documents from the higher echelons in Moscow, breathing wrath and full of threats levelled at the administration of the Hermitage. Properly speaking, the very fact that government executives — and not the Museum authorities as originally planned — were invested with the right to withdraw museum items, was in itself a sign of a lack of confidence in the loyalty of the Hermitage.

Attempts were made to address protests and send appeals to the powers that be. Prominent scholars, like Academician Sergei Oldenburg, pleaded against the sales. Letters were showered on Stalin from every side, some of them from the Hermitage. But no answers came until things were ripe for a change.

The sales ceased in the early 1930s. This was due to several reasons. Viewed from the Hermitage standpoints, it looked like an answer to a prayer of Iosif Orbeli, Head of the Oriental Department. He wrote a letter to Stalin, informing him that the Antikvariat, a body engaged in the sales of art objects, extended its claims to the holdings of the Oriental Department. The danger threatening Oriental treasures may have

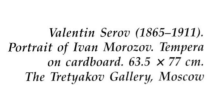

*Valentin Serov (1865–1911).
Portrait of Ivan Morozov. Tempera
on cardboard. 63.5 × 77 cm.
The Tretyakov Gallery, Moscow*

touched the heart of the Caucasian. In addition, the letter reached Stalin through the mediation of Orbeli's friend, Abel Enukidze: it was sure to be presented with comments favourable to the sender. The answer came almost immediately. It said, "Esteemed Comrade Orbeli: Inspection has shown the claims of the Antikvariat to have no foundation. In this connection, the People's Commissariat for Foreign Trade and its expert bodies have been instructed by proper authorities to keep clear of the Oriental Department of the Hermitage. I think the question may be regarded as settled. Respectfully, Iosif Stalin. 5.IX.32."

The sales stopped; the items already withdrawn began to return from auction storerooms and antiquity shops. It goes without saying that no letters or complaints could by themselves have affected the course of government policy. But they may have fallen on favourable soil, prepared by increasing discontent with the sales, of which the proceeds were low, but which excited universal protests. Anyhow, the principal goal had already been reached: Russia's "friends" helped to open for it a door to the world market of commodities and credits.

There is no doubt that the sales of Hermitage treasures were a crime against national culture. Yet those who initiated them must not be considered to have been complete idiots. The breakthrough into the world market meant a possibility to import and master the newest technologies which turned out to be of no small importance during the 1941–45 War. It may be argued whether or not the expense was really adequate to the gain. One thing, however, is clear: that the Hermitage paid with its heart's blood for Russia's economical and political advance of the 1930s; and that the country's debt to the Museum has not been discharged to this day.

Other measures undertaken by government bodies in control of museum activities were also fraught with dramatic consequences for the Hermitage. The plan for transferring the evacuated Hermitage pictures to the former Alexander III Museum of Fine Arts, which was to become the "Moscow Hermitage", had been formed when they were still in the new capital; but the first attack had been beaten off, and the pictures returned to Petrograd. However, in 1924, People's Commissariat for Education decreed that the Museum of Fine Arts should be restructured and its holdings increased by the addition of original works, mainly paintings, from other museums. Involved in this restructuring were the Moscow Rumiantsev Museum and the Tretyakov Gallery, also in Moscow, whence came canvases by Western European masters. Collections of the picture galleries of Petrograd palace museums, which had been closed down, were also to be divided between the Hermitage and the Moscow Museum of Fine Arts. A special commission was set up for the "redistribution" of the art works. As a result of its activity, the Hermitage picture gallery received 95 canvases from the Yusupov collection, and lost 78 paintings from its own: they went to the Moscow museum. Until 1930, 70 pictures formerly belonging to the Hermitage and now classed by Hermitage scholars as "of doubtful ownership", remained in Leningrad. There were paintings by Perugino, Rubens, Rembrandt, and Poussin among the number.

In 1948, the Hermitage received a rich collection of modern Western European paintings from the Moscow Museum of Modern Western European Art, a gallery unique of its kind in Russia, which had been closed down even before the war. A certain number of paintings were then transferred to the Hermitage; but it was only after the war that the bulk of the museum's holdings was divided between the Hermitage and the Pushkin Museum of Fine Arts in Moscow. This transaction may be regarded as a sort of compensation for the hundreds of Old Master paintings withdrawn from the Hermitage in the 1920s. The collection, incorporating Western European 19th- and early 20th-century paintings, consisted of works assembled and owned by two great Moscow art lovers, Sergei Shchukin and Ivan Morozov.

In our present-day opinion, any instance of destroying the unity of an art collection or a properly-built museum may, and probably should, be condemned as an act of barbarism. But in the case under discussion, the division of museum holdings proved to be salutary for the collections. During the post-war years, all modern art, far from being appreciated, was viewed by the authorities as highly pernicious to the dominant ideology. The closing down of the museum might well be followed by other acts of persecution. It is known that there was a plan for disseminating the collections among small provincial museums. The pictures might also be sold to foreign buyers: there were negotiations going on to this effect, and in the 1930s, several pictures had actually been sold. Last of all, the canvases ran the risk of being physically destroyed.

Having once been incorporated in officially recognized museums like the Hermitage and the Pushkin Museum of Fine Arts, the masterpieces of Monet, Cézanne, Matisse, and Picasso were immune against any attempts at their safety. Moreover, they were returned to the viewer. What could not be done in a separate museum, was possible in the broad context of an exhibition illustrating the history of world culture, where these works appeared as part of cultural revolution, although a "bad" part. And indeed, in the 1950s and '60s, the "ideologically hostile" paintings gradually found their way into exhibition rooms, both in the Hermitage and the Pushkin Museum of Fine Arts. The "Second Floor" of the Hermitage became a place of pilgrimage to the intelligentsia; and it was there that many excellent painters made their first acquaintance with the modern art of the West, formerly hardly available to the general viewer.

World War II brought with it the worst danger the Hermitage had to face in the whole course of its existence. The Museum might be razed to the ground; or it might be completely looted. A German force was at the approaches to Leningrad, and again the Hermitage had to evacuate its treasures. The Museum was ready for this. Hardly a week had passed since the beginning of the hostilities when the first train with Hermitage collections in it started for Sverdlovsk (now Ekaterinburg) in the Urals. Another train followed; but after that the way was blocked, and the crates prepared for shipment by a third train remained in the Hermitage. The main bulk of the Museum's treasures stayed in Sverdlovsk until the end of the war, under the vigilant care of Sverdlovsk people and a group of Hermitage workers in charge. Not a single item was found missing.

Meanwhile, strenuous work was going on in the Hermitage itself. Every effort was made to protect the remaining collections and to shelter objects of cultural value brought over for safe keeping from other Leningrad institutions and from palace museums in the environs. Exposed to all the horrors of the blockade, cruelly suffering from cold and permanent gnawing hunger, Hermitage people did conservation work, protected the Museum's buildings from incendiary bombs and artillery shells, and did their best to save its splendid interiors from the destructive action of the wind, snow, and rain. The basement was fitted out as an air-raid shelter; it preserved the lives of many representatives of Leningrad intelligentsia.

Setting an example of discipline and high morale — those main factors necessary for survival — the Museum never for a moment gave up its work of preserving and developing national culture. Research and educational activity continued. A memorial confer-

Xan Krohn (1882–1959). Portrait of Sergei Shchukin. 1916. Oil on canvas. 190 × 86.3 cm. The Hermitage

ence was held in honour of the great Oriental poet Nizami, and another in that of Navoï (in their home countries, Azerbaijan and Uzbekistan, the anniversary celebrations were postponed till after the war). For the soldiers who visited the Museum, perfectly surrealist lecture tours were given: they were guided round the bare rooms hung with empty frames, and listened to the lecturer's descriptions of the paintings they used to contain.

After the lifting of the blockade and the hard-won victory, the Hermitage began to revive; the breaches from bombs and shells were gradually repaired; evacuated collections came back home; the old exhibitions were restored and new ones mounted.

In the post-war years, the Hermitage was charged with an extra responsibility: *viz.*, the storing and preservation of a certain portion of art collections brought over from Germany after its defeat. The Soviet government saw them as a possible compensation for the untold losses inflicted by Fascist aggression on the artistic and cultural heritage of the nations of the USSR.

The reception and preservation of these collections, which were to be hidden from the public eye, and yet required the utmost care, was a heavy burden for the Museum, whose immediate duty, the restoration of its own stores and its own expositions, was felt to be of paramount importance. Nevertheless, all items entrusted to the Museum for safe keeping were preserved in perfect order. Now, it is common knowledge that art works which remained in German territory after the end of the war and were not carried away and placed in museums, were either stolen, or lost, or else destroyed; only a small part of them came up, from time to time, for sale in the black market.

In the early months of 1958, the Soviet government restored to Germany its salvaged art treasures. A show was mounted in the Hermitage, which gave an idea of the work done in their conservation and restoration. The exhibits included the monumental Pergamum Altar and the famous sculptural portrait of Nefertiti, a Queen of Ancient Egypt. At an earlier date, the Hermitage had restored to Poland a collection of objects coming from its territory. Polish art works were transferred to their home country in the course of the following years as well.

A certain number of other items which reached the Hermitage due to the fortunes of war are still kept in the stores by government order. They are treated with the same loving care and attention as the Museum's own things. Whatever the final government decision may be, the Museum workers are even today doing everything they can to have these works placed on display and let them resume their cultural mission, regardless of who may eventually be pronounced to be their rightful owner.

All through the years, from the 18th century to our own day, Hermitage collections have been enriched by gifts from the Museum's sympathizers and friends. Until the revolution of 1917, members of the Imperial family were the Museum's chief patrons. Their concern for the growth of the collections took different forms. Apart from many widely known instances, there was one comparatively little known. It was the Crown Prince Nicholas's (afterwards Nicholas II) contribution to the Japanese collection after his visit to Japan in 1891.

Nicholas, who developed quite a passion for Japanese culture, bought a great variety of art objects.* He also received, as a matter of course, a lot of diplomatic presents, mostly preserved in the Hermitage to this day. Of these, one of the most remarkable is a magnificent brocade carpet, a masterwork by the celebrated Japanese 19th-century weaver Kawashima

* The author is greatly indebted to Mikhail Uspensky of the Hermitage Oriental Department for providing relevant materials.

Jimbei, who used a special technique of his own invention. His technique combined European and Far Eastern traditions in weaving. The design shows a scene of dog hunting — a popular Samurai contest — in a traditional ornamental border incorporating motifs of Japanese and Russian state arms: chrysanthemums and double-headed eagles. The carpet of great intrinsic value was presented to Nicholas at the close of his visit, probably by way of apology for an attempt on his life, which took place in the town of Otsu. The Orthodox Christian Mission in Japan made to the Crown Prince a gift of an icon of *The Resurrection* painted by a Japanese artist Yamachita Rin; it is interesting to note that she had had a two-year course of training in the art of painting in Russia. The composition of the icon was not the artist's own, but a reproduction of a Russian original (see p. 123).

The Japanese collection includes one more remarkable gift made to the Hermitage, although it is of a different kind. Sergei Varshavsky, a well-known Petersburg art collector, a friend of the Museum and author of several books on its history and collections, willed to the Hermitage a rich assortment of netsuke, Japanese minor sculpture, a branch of Japanese art which is highly popular in Europe.

Today collectors' gifts form one of the principal sources of new accessions to the Museum's collections. The Hermitage holds in high esteem the memory of men who thought it their duty to make the results of their life-long collecting a part of the Hermitage holdings. There have been a multitude of such donations in the Museum's history. Special mention should be made of some of the latest among them: an excellent collection of Oriental glyptics, assembled by the Soviet mineralogist Georgy Lemmlein, and a collection of objects of Russian art presented by Grigory Dushin.

One of the most touching gifts came from Lydia Delectorskaya, residing in France, who had long been a secretary of the great Henri Matisse. She gave to the Museum a large number of Matisse's paintings, sculptures, drawings, and books designed and illustrated by him.

Many artists active today think it an honour to have their works received by the Hermitage as gifts. A beautiful collection of modern Italian sculptures has been formed of the rich donations from such famous sculptors as Francesco Messina, Giacomo Manzu, Emilio Greco, and Vincenzo Crocetti.

Interior in Ivan Morozov's mansion.
Photograph. The Pushkin Museum
of Fine Arts, Moscow

Jan van Eyck (about 1422–1441).
Left: The Crucifixion.
Right: The Last Judgment.
Tempera and oil on canvas,
transferred from wood.
© The Metropolitan Museum of Art,
Fletcher Fund, 1933
Formerly the Hermitage collection

Raphael (1483–1520). Saint George
and the Dragon. C. 1506.
Oil on panel. 285 × 215 cm.
© National Gallery of Art,
Washington
Andrew W. Mellon Collection
Formerly the Hermitage collection

Interior in Sergei Shchukin's mansion. Photograph. The Pushkin
Museum of Fine Arts, Moscow

Sandro Botticelli (1444/1445–1510).
The Adoration of the Magi.
Early 1480s. Tempera and oil
on panel. 70.2 x 104.2 cm.
© National Gallery of Art,
Washington
Andrew W. Mellon Collection
Formerly the Hermitage collection

Rembrandt Harmensz van Rijn
(1606–1669). Pallas. 1663.
Oil on canvas. Lisbon, Museum
Calouste Gulbenkian
Formerly the Hermitage collection

Perugino (about 1448–1524).
The Crucifixion with the Virgin,
Saint John, Saint Jerome, and Saint
Mary Magdalene. C. 1485. Triptych.
Oil on panel transferred to canvas.
© National Gallery of Art,
Washington
Andrew W. Mellon Collection
Formerly the Hermitage collection

Rembrandt Harmensz van Rijn,
Workshop (1606–1669). Possibly
Fabritius, Carel (C. 1622–1654).
*A Girl with a Broom. Probably
begun 1646/1648 and completed 1651.
Oil on canvas. 107 × 91 cm.*
© *National Gallery of Art,
Washington*
*Andrew W. Mellon Collection
Formerly the Hermitage collection*

Rembrandt Harmensz van Rijn
(1606–1669). *Portrait of a Lady
with an Ostrich-Feather Fan.
C. 1658–60. Oil on canvas
transferred to canvas. 99.5 × 83 cm.*
© *National Gallery of Art,
Washington. Widener Collection
Formerly the Hermitage collection*

170

Nicolas Poussin (1594–1665).
The Birth of Venus. 1635 or 1636.
Oil on canvas. 97.1 × 107.9 cm.
© Philadelphia Museum of Art:
The George W. Elkins Collection
Formerly the Hermitage collection

Jean-Antoine Houdon (1741–1828).
Diana. Marble. Lisbon, Museu
Calouste Gulbenkian. From the
Hermitage collection

Hubert Robert (1733–1808).
Versailles. Oil on canvas. Lisbon,
Museu Calouste Gulbenkian.
From the Hermitage collection

175

Figure of an eagle. By Master Sulei-
man. 796–797. Iran. Bronze (brass).
Height 38 cm. The Hermitage. From
the city of Grozny

Pot. By Muhammad ibn Abu
al-vahid and Mas'ud ibn Ahmad
al-naqqash. 1163. Iran (Gerat).
Bronze. Height 18.5 cm.
The Hermitage. From the
Alexei Bobrinsky collection

Hilt of a sabre. Late 18th – early
19th centuries. Iran. Gold, gems.
The Hermitage. From the Catherine
Palace Museum, Pushkin

Aquamanile in the form of a cow.
By Ali ibn Muhammad ibn
Abu-l-Kasim al-naqqash. 1206.
Iran. Bronze. 35 × 31.5 × 14 cm.
The Hermitage. From the
Alexei Bobrinsky collection

Hilt of a dagger. Late 17th – early
18th centuries. Gold, enamel.
The Hermitage. From the Tsarskoye
Selo Arsenal (as part of the Peter
the Great collection)

176

Jug. 17th century. India. Gold, gems. Height 28.8 cm. The Hermitage. Gift of the Nadir-shah embassy, 1741

The outer surface of the gold jug is embellished with rubies, emeralds, diamonds and pearls; its inner surface is silver.

Jug. 8th–9th centuries. Iran. Bronze (brass). Height 40.5 cm. The Hermitage. From the Alexei Bobrinsky collection

This jug in the form of a bird of prey belongs to the same type of vessel as the Figure of an Eagle.

Daikoku with a Box and a Rat. By Toji. Second half of the 19th century. Japan. Edo School. Ivory. 6.4 × 2.4 cm. The Hermitage. From the Sergei Varshavsky collection

Tengu. By Masa Shumin (Shumin III). Mid-19th century. Japan. Edo School. Wood, horn. 4.4 × 3.5 cm. The Hermitage. From the Sergei Varshavsky collection

Onna-daruma (daruma in the form of a woman). Mid-19th century. Japan. Osaka School. Wood, ivory. 4.6 × 2.4 cm. The Hermitage. From the Sergei Varshavsky collection

A Blind Man Lifting a Stone. First half of the 19th century. Japan. Edo School. Wood. 3.4 × 4 cm. The Hermitage. From the Sergei Varshavsky collection

He-he er-xian (immortal twins: unity and consent). By Tomochika Yamaguchi II. Mid-19th century. Japan. Edo School. Ivory. 3.3 × 4 cm. The Hermitage. From the Sergei Varshavsky collection

Hotei and Two Boys Karako. By Takehara Chikko. Late 19th – first half of the 20th centuries. Japan. Osaka School. Ivory. 4 × 3.4 cm. The Hermitage. From the Sergei Varshavsky collection

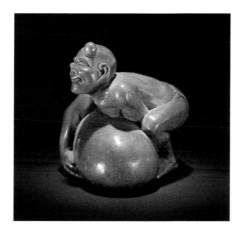

The netsuke is a traditional Japanese art, a truly national form of miniature sculpture. The range of netsuke subjects provides a rare chance to gain an insight into Japanese life between the 17th and 19th centuries. These small-size figures carved in wood or ivory tell us about mythological, religious, literary, or historical personages that were popular in Japan at that time, as well as about people's everyday life. They vividly demonstrate that the best beloved personages were not the buddhas and bodhisattvas whose statues appeared in temples, but the divinities known as the Seven Gods of Happiness. These gods of different origin (Buddhist, Shinto, Taoist) were worshipped as harbingers of health, longevity and peace, the most popular among them being Daikoku and Hotei. Daikoku is the Japanese adaptation of an Indian deity — a fierce guardian of faith; in Japan it became a god of good luck and wealth. His attributes are huge sacks of rice, a hammer forging wealth, and rats — all symbolizing happiness and well-being. Hotei, who was derived from the Indian buddha Maitreya, has a similar symbolic meaning: he was thought to have the ability to grant happiness and to ensure a life free of troubles and hardships. Equally popular were Taoist deities epitomizing the idea of longevity or immortality, for instance, the Immortal Twins of Unity and Consent (He-he er-xian), the subject rarely encountered in netsukes. Another typical figure from popular beliefs is Tengu — a mythological creature of Chinese origin. Netsuke subjects have for the most part a well-wishing or protective meaning.

Vincent Van Gogh (1853–1890).
Cottages with Thatched Roofs.
1890. Oil on canvas. 60 × 73 cm.
The Hermitage. From the Ivan
Morozov collection, Moscow

Pierre Auguste Renoir (1841–1919).
Girl with a Fan. 1881. Oil on canvas.
65 × 50 cm. The Hermitage. From the
Ivan Morozov collection, Moscow

181

Claude Monet (1840–1926). Lady
in the Garden (Sainte-Adresse).
1867. Oil on canvas. 80 × 90 cm.
The Hermitage. From the Sergei
Shchukin collection, Moscow

Paul Gauguin (1848–1903). Woman
Holding a Fruit. 1893. Oil on canvas.
92 × 73 cm. The Hermitage. From the
Ivan Morozov collection, Moscow

Paul Cézanne (1839–1906). Great Pine near Aix. Late 1890s. Oil on canvas. 72 × 91 cm. The Hermitage. From the Ivan Morozov collection, Moscow

Camille Pissarro (1830–1903).
Boulevard Montmartre in Paris.
1897. Oil on canvas. 73 × 92 cm.
The Hermitage. From the Mikhail
Riabushinsky collection, Moscow

Maurice de Vlaminck (1876–1958).
Town on the Shore of a Lake. About
1907. Oil on canvas. 80 × 99 cm.
The Hermitage. From the Sergei
Shchukin collection, Moscow

Cornelis van Dongen (1877–1968).
Red Dancer. About 1907. Oil on
canvas. 99 × 80 cm. The Hermitage.
From the Nikolai Riabushinsky
collection

Paul Signac (1863–1935). Harbour
in Marseilles. 1906. Oil on canvas.
46 × 55 cm. The Hermitage. From the
Ivan Morozov collection, Moscow

Albert Marquet (1875–1947).
Seascape (Naples). 1909. Oil on can-
vas. 61.5 × 80 cm. The Hermitage.
From the Ivan Morozov collection,
Moscow

Henri Matisse (1869–1954).
The Dance. 1910. Oil on canvas.
260 × 391 cm. The Hermitage.
From the Sergei Shchukin collection,
Moscow

189

Sylvester Shchedrin (1791–1830).
Grotto in Sorrento. 1826. Oil on
canvas. 25.4 × 19 cm. The Hermitage.
Gift of E. Shapiro

Henri Matisse (1869–1954). Portrait
of Lydia Delectorskaya. 1947. Oil on
canvas. 64.3 × 49.7 cm. The Hermit-
age. Gift of Lydia Delectorskaya

193

*Icon: St Gregory the Thaumaturgist.
12th century. Byzantium. Tempera on
panel. 81 × 53 cm. The Hermitage.
Brought from a monastery on Mount
Athos by Piotr Sevastyanov in 1860*

*The art of Byzantium exerted a deep in-
fluence on both Western European and
Russian painting. Here is one of the
masterpieces of Byzantine art.*

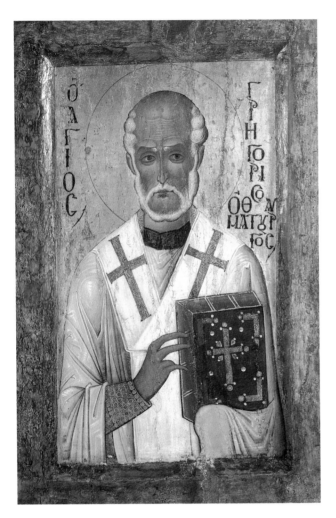

*Nectarius Kuliuksin. St. John
the Theologian in Silence. 1679.
Workshop of the Kirillo-Belozersky
Monastery. 109 × 85 × 3.5 cm.
The Hermitage. From Arkhangelsk
Region. 1960*

*One of St John's hands touches his lips
(the sign of silence), while behind his
back is an angel in glory (the sign of
divine wisdom).*

Kirill Golovachevsky. 1735–1823.
Portrait of S. Krenitsyn. 1750s. Oil on
canvas. 60 × 50 cm. The Hermitage.
From the G. Dushin collection

Mina Kolokolnikov (about 1708 –
about 1792). Portrait of Alexei
Vasilyev. About 1761. Oil on
canvas. 63 × 51 cm. The Hermitage.
From the G. Dushin collection

The Winter Palace of Peter the Great
found during the restoration of the
Hermitage Theatre. Peter the Great
(the so-called "Wax Persona").
18th century. Height of the figure
204 cm; armchair 114 × 80 × 58 cm.
The Hermitage

The Winter Palace of Peter the Great.
Interior

*Menshikov Palace (Branch of the
Hermitage: Department of Russian
Culture). Walnut Study. 18th century*

Carlo Bartolommeo Rastrelli
(1675–1744). Portrait of Alexander
Menshikov. Bronze. Height 122.5 cm.
The Hermitage

Alexander Menshikov (1673–1729) was
a powerful statesman and Peter the
Great's favourite companion and chief
adviser; he was also the first Governor
of St Petersburg.

The Gothic Library in the Winter
Palace. Architect Alexander
Krasovsky. 1890s

Dish: Bird Carrying a Goddess.
First half of the 8th century. Iran.
Silver. Diam. 22 cm. The Hermitage.
Found in Perm

Archaeological Explorations as a Source of the Museum's Holdings

Ages ago, in the 5th century B.C., Herodotus, the "Father of History", in Book IV of his great work, described a land inhabited by Scythians, nomadic tribes of mounted warriors and skilful agriculturalists. They dwelt in the steppes of the northern Black Sea coast area. Their tombs, with tall mounds raised over them, formed an even more characteristic feature of the region's landscape than did the barrows in the Urals and Siberia. For the most part, these tombs had been rifled in antiquity: which was the first wave of successful grave robberies. In the modern period, the local population took to plundering the burials with a zeal not inferior to that of the ancient robbers. Owing to this, hardly any materials from Scythian burial mounds ever found their way to archaeological collections or museums.

In the reign of Catherine II, the foundress of the Hermitage, Russia finally established her dominion over the southern steppes, won over from Turkey. It was then that the first archaeological discoveries were made in the region. In 1763, at the command of General Melgunov, a barrow called Litoi was excavated. The finds — a gold gorytus, some eagle-shaped plaques, and quaint animal figures — were brought to the capital and placed in the *Kunstkammer*. Subsequently they passed on to the Hermitage. These finds, known as the Melgunov Treasure, were so called not after the place of discovery but after the name of the General who had given the command, although he had never so much as set foot on the site. By contrast, all other archaeological findings entered the history of archaeology under the geographical names of the findspots, for all that their discoverers and excavators were most worthy and learned men, fully deserving to be remembered by posterity. (In justice to the posterity, it should be said that they have not been forgotten.) The name given to the first of the excavated barrows reflected a notable feature of the early phase in the study of southern Russia's antiquities. They were sought out and dug by "generals": important government officials, civil as well as military. Their efforts brought to our knowledge the first Scythian relics, along with the remnants of cities and necropoli of their neighbours, Greek colonists.

The first to attract special attention was Panticapaeum, a town once situated on the site of modern Kerch, a great military and commercial centre of the Crimea. The governors of Kerch and their officials set up a regular hunt after antiquities, buying them from the locals and encouraging small-scale diggings. The finds were deposited in local museums and demonstrated to visitors, one of whom happened to be the Emperor Alexander I.

In 1828, Ivan Stempkovsky was appointed Governor of Kerch. He had developed an interest in antiquities back in 1814, while in Paris with the victorious Russian army. He was indefatigable in encouraging interest in archaeological explorations and collecting of ancient objects. In 1830, the military needed building stone for the construction of the barracks. It was decided to quarry it at the spot where the local people used to obtain it: the Kul-Oba hill. The builders found blocks of roughly dressed stone made into a huge burial structure. The quarrying of building materials turned into archaeological excavations. Soon a large funerary chamber was opened. As usual in such cases, it had been visited by robbers. But this time fate was kind to Stempkovsky and Paul Dubrux, Director of the excavations. By the side of the main burial chamber was found a smaller one, which had happily escaped the attention of robbers. The two skeletons lying there were literally strewn with gold objects. And although part of the treasure was stolen from the unguarded chamber during the night, the number of precious finds was enormous, quite stunning.

The grave goods were not only fabulously rich but also exceptionally interesting to the historian. They presented so striking a picture of the convergence of Hellenic and Scythian cultures that at first the scholars could not agree about the national identity of the "owner" of the burial. Who was he: a Scythian, or a Bosporan Greek? One of the most remarkable artifacts was the famous electrum vessel with scenes of Scythian life. The scenes have been comparatively recently interpreted as illustrating a myth of the Scythians electing a king to rule over them. The grave goods also included some gold costume plaques showing two warriors in the act of drinking from a single cup. The subject illustrated a custom described by Herodotus: two Scythians became blood brothers by drinking blood from the same cup. There were also torques with the terminals shaped as figures of mounted Scythians, and similarly decorated gold overlays. Contrasted to these were artifacts of a different kind, such as the gold temple pendant with a miniature head of Athena, reproducing that of Phidias's statue, crafted for the Acropolis in 438 B.C.

This curious repertory of grave goods opened up a new, highly important branch of research, first suggested by Siberian discoveries, and dealing with the problem of the unity of Eurasian cultures, and the links existing between them.

The Kul-Oba treasure was brought to St Petersburg and presented with due pomp to the Emperor Nicholas I. The brilliant results of the first Russian archaeological excavations were received as a national triumph.

These events gave a new impetus to the already active search for antiquities in the Black Sea coast area. Mighty barrows were opened in the presence of crowds of enthusiastic spectators. Although almost always found to have been plundered in antiquity, they still yielded numerous finds. The Hermitage became the principal centre for the preservation and study of the most important finds. Up to this day, investigations into the archaeology of the antique Black Sea coast area and Scythian culture have formed one of the main branches of the Museum's scientific research.

In 1852, when the Hermitage became a public museum and its collections were arranged in a new building, specially fitted for museum purposes, a separate hall was assigned for the display of materials from the Black Sea coast area — the antiquities of the Cimmerian Bosporus. In 1859, a part of the Siberian collection of Peter the Great was also placed there.

The year 1859 was marked by the creation of the Imperial Archaeological Commission as a coordinating body directing the acquisition, study, and publication of antiquities. The Commission conducted excavations.

Most of the findings eventually reached the Hermitage. The Commission took care to make its first diggings a success. The object chosen was a twenty-metre high barrow on the bank of a small river Chertomlyk, flowing into the Dnieper. The barrow was believed to conceal untold treasures, if the legends widely circulating among the local population were to be trusted. As in all similar cases, the funerary chamber uncovered by the well-known archaeologist Ivan Zabelin who directed the works, was found to be empty. One of the robbers who had plundered it was destined never again to see the light of day. His skeleton, the oil lamp he had held in his hand, and his burden of the loot were discovered by the archaeologists in the entrance shaft where he had been trapped by a fall of earth.

Except for this first piece of ill luck, fortune favoured the excavators. The barrow appeared to contain several more burials, each accompanied by a rich assortment of grave goods. It was there that one of the most celebrated Hermitage possessions, the Chertomlyk vase, was found: a silver vessel, probably used to contain mare's milk, and decorated with applied vegetative and animal motifs, and — last but not least — masterly representations of Scythians and their famous horses.

Concurrently, excavations were conducted on the sites of antique cities of the Black Sea coast area, Panticapaeum and Olbia. They yielded large numbers of remarkable artifacts, which had, in addition to their artistic merit, considerable archaeological value, for they helped to systematize materials recovered before. Frequent clearings and meticulous analysis of the layers enabled Russian scholars to establish the relative and absolute chronology of the levels, and to date the links between the Greek towns and the Scythian world. Especially noteworthy was the indefatigable activity of Boris Farmakovsky, Director of the excavations at Olbia. The study of the many sites whose exploration was started by the Imperial Archaeological Commission, has been continued to this day by Hermitage expeditions.

Among the grave goods of a rich Greek woman buried at Phanagoria in the 5th century B.C. were found three painted

Boris Piotrovsky during excavations at Karmir-Blur. Photograph

ceramic figure vessels. One of them, quite amazing for the mastery of its execution and the delicacy of its colouring, is traditionally known by the name of the Phanagorian Sphinx; another represents a singing Siren; and the third, Aphrodite sprung from sea-foam.

A Greek burial near Theodosia yielded the celebrated Theodosian earrings, a masterpiece of antique goldwork, dating from the 4th century B.C. The goldsmith managed to arrange within the disc in their top part the chariot of the goddess Nike, drawn by four horses and flanked by two minute figures of warriors. He spattered his work with a profusion of rosettes, palmettes, garlands, and flowers. The crescent and other details belonging to the lower part of the earrings are set with the tiniest imaginable granules of gold. Excavations on the site where the earrings come from were financed by the prominent Russian painter Ivan Aivazovsky, a resident of Theodosia, who did much to promote the study of antiquities in the land he loved.

The personality of the great archaeologist Nikolai I. Veselovsky deserves special notice. He occupies a place apart in the history of Scythian research in Russia, so rich in brilliant discoveries. Archaeology is a peculiar branch of science. It requires more than just talent, hard work, and skill: essential to success here is luck. Veselovsky was fortunate in possessing all the necessary qualifications which ensure success, including luck. He made several remarkable discoveries, which marked high points in the history of Russian archaeology. In 1897, he excavated the famous Maikop barrow in the North Caucasus, the burial of a tribal chieftain dating back to the 3rd millennium B.C. The grave goods from this barrow are preserved in the Gold Room of the Hermitage. They are of the greatest interest not only for their specific charm but also for the wide range of historico-cultural associations they call up.

The Scythian barrow near the Kostromskaya village was also excavated by Veselovsky. It was here that he found the gold overlay in the form of a stag figure, which served as the centrepiece of a shield. The stag is shown in the middle of a flying jump. Widely known the world over, this masterpiece has acquired in the public mind the significance of a symbol of Scythian art and, moreover, even of the Hermitage itself.

Veselovsky completed the excavations of the Kelermes Barrow, well-nigh destroyed by the barbarous diggings of "pioneer" treasure hunters. There he discovered a celebrated Scythian masterpiece, the gold panther plaque, another famous Hermitage treasure. Veselovsky's run of luck was crowned in the early years of the 20th century by the excavation of the Solokha Barrow. Situated on the left bank of the Dnieper, this huge mound had long intrigued the archaeologists; but it was not before 1912 that Veselovsky could start the diggings. The first burial chamber he uncovered had been robbed, but he persevered with the work. Finally was discovered a royal Scythian funerary chamber, perfectly intact and filled with gold ornaments, decorated weapons, and other artifacts of great beauty and value. Generally known are the Solokha comb crested with figures of fighting warriors and the ritual bowl with a masterfully executed frieze of running animals.

The Solokha discoveries were followed by those made near the Elizavetinskaya village. A sudden end was put to archaeological activity by the workings of history. The revolution of 1917 broke out and a civil war came in its wake. The next sequence of rich Scythian tombs was excavated only in the 1960s. The territory then belonged to the Ukrainian SSR, and so the findings never reached the Hermitage.

However, archaeological work, interrupted by the troublous times, was gradually resumed. The diggings of the post-revolutionary period, including those conducted, or participated in, by Hermitage scholars, yielded important results and laid the foundations of the Museum's world-famous collections.

Now the Hermitage Department of the Art and Culture of the Antique World carries on archaeological work on a large scale. Particularly remarkable results have been achieved by its expeditions to Berezan Island, Chersonesus, and Nymphaeum. The excavations, conducted systematically over a number of years, enabled the scholars to recon-

Head of a Woman. 1st century. Eastern shore of the Mediterranean. Glass. Height 3.5 cm. The Hermitage. From Nymphaeum. 1983

In 1983, in the course of excavations in the Roman sections of Nymphaeum, the Hermitage archaeologists found a fragment of a miniature statue — the head of a young woman with a diadem made of transparent colour glass. The head shows a close affinity to the sculptural portraits and representations on coins of the Empress Livia.

struct in detail the picture of the cities' planning, their development, and their functional evolution. Chersonesus provides a good example of this. Its centuries-long history has been traced stage by stage, with periods of transition documented archaeologically. For instance, the shift from the paganism of antiquity to Christianity was reflected in the secondary use of slabs from a Roman sarcophagus, employed as building material in the construction of a Christian church.

Not only did archaeologists discover a wealth of beautiful art objects; but they also found the remains of workshops where these artifacts were manufactured along with other objects of simpler type intended for everyday use. The metalworkers', glass makers', and dyers' shops, the wineries and fish-salters' shops testified to the daily occupations of the population and helped to visualize the busy life of the city's streets. The finds recovered in Berezan, including splendid examples of classic Greek art, unearthed side-by-side with routine productions for household use, provided important data on the beginnings of Greek colonization of the Black Sea coast area, which must be referred to the 7th century B.C.

Impressive results have been obtained by the expedition to Nymphaeum in the Crimea. The site of an ancient city with its numerous houses, its artificial terraces, and antique wineries, was thoroughly explored. Special attention was given to religious buildings: a sanctuary of the goddess Demeter, another one dedicated to deities of the underworld, and a temple to patron gods of navigation. The vast necropolis yielded valuable evidence on the structure of the city's population and on their religious practices. It was also found to be rich in beautiful examples of antique art, which are now in the Hermitage collection. Of considerable artistic interest and the greatest historical value is the large *sgraffito* picture of a ship, accompanied by numerous smaller scratched contours of ships and other graffiti, all of them represented on the inner wall of a Nymphaean 3rd-century B.C. temple, over its fresco decoration of alternating bands of different colours.

The excavations of the barrows at Pazyryk in the Altai mountains, South Siberia, led to sensational discoveries. Owing to specific natural conditions, objects of such perishable materials as wood, textile, and leather, had not only survived but were found to be in an amazingly good state of preservation. The repertory of finds was also unique for its wealth and completeness. The Altai tombs were topped with boulders, which let water penetrate inside the burials. In winter this water froze into ice, which never thawed out completely during the short and cold summer. Thus a layer of permanent frost formed inside each mound, creating ideal conditions for the conservation of the burials.

The excavations at Pazyryk were conducted in the 1920s and later in the 1940s. They were directed by Sergei Rudenko and Mikhail Griaznov, respectively. Excellently preserved trunk coffins were found (an example is to be seen in the Hermitage exhibition). One of the coffins contained the remains of two persons, a chief and his wife. Outside the burial chamber were compartments with remnants of horses and component parts of a dismantled waggon. The waggon has been reassembled and is on display. Among other accessories was a tent and an enormous felt rug. Decorated with appliqué in vivid colours, the rug showed the figure of a goddess enthroned and holding out a branch of the Tree of Life to a dark-haired rider. The tent poles were once topped by figures of swans in black and white felt.

Permanent frost ensured the preservation of the shapes and colouring of other objects as well: clothes, footwear, fur cloaks, and musical instruments. The horse trappings included some astonishing specimens of horse's ritual headdresses shaped as stag heads with antlers. Pazyryk Barrow V yielded one of the most remarkable finds, a worsted pile carpet adorned with figures of stags, horses, and gryphons. It was made in Asia Minor and is datable to a period between the 6th and the 4th centuries B.C., as are all Pazyryk barrows. This is one of the most ancient examples of works of its kind predating the earliest known pile carpets by no less than

*Excavations at Nymphaeum.
Photograph*

a millennium and a half, since they refer to a time not before the 13th century.

The Pazyryk barrows had been visited by robbers in antiquity. All artifacts of precious metals had been stolen. And nevertheless the remaining grave goods extracted by the archaeologists of our days are still far superior for their artistic value and their scientific importance to much of what had been known from previous excavations. Stylistically, the lively and extraordinarily expressive animal figures and ornamental motifs from Altaic burials are obviously akin, on the one hand, to objects from the Siberian collection of Peter the Great, and on the other, to Scythian artifacts from South Russia. The findings from Pazyryk are of key importance to the study of the problem of Scythian cultural unity. They serve to knit into a single whole the results of numerous preceding and subsequent diggings conducted over the wide expanses of Eurasia.

Another major achievement of Russian archaeology, the discovery of Urartu, most dramatically confirmed the existence of links between the Scythian world and Ancient Orient. Assyria's rival from the 8th to the 6th centuries B.C., the state of Urartu, dominating vast territories in Asia Minor and the South Caucasus, fell under the blows of its neighbours. In this Scythians played a special part. Materials from the excavations which lasted for over 30 years enabled the scholars to reconstruct a detailed picture of Scythian attack on the Urartian fortress Teisbaini and this stronghold's final destruction. The data of the excavation throw light on Scythian methods of warfare, employed in this and possibly many other campaigns. The works, conducted by a joint expedition of the Hermitage and the Armenia SSR Academy of Sciences on the Karmir-Blur hill near Erevan, were directed throughout the whole of the 30 years' period by Boris Piotrovsky, who ended his career as Director of the Hermitage.

The diggings on Karmir-Blur which yielded a tremendous wealth of first-rate finds, brought Urartu out of its state of semi-oblivion and gave it a worthy place on the pages of world history. Much preliminary work by collectors and scholars preceded the expedition. As early as 1895, the Mil-

itary Governor of Erevan, Major Koliubakin, presented to the Hermitage a few bronze figurines and bells picked up by some Kurds in a rock cave on the bank of the Araxes. Only years later they were defined as objects of Urartian origin. A cuneiform text with the name of the Urartian king Argistis was found on one of the bells. Subsequently, other finds from the region came to the Hermitage through certain antiquity dealers. They were Urartian figurines which turned out to be fragments from a throne, whose other parts were disseminated among a number of world museums. Eventually, Russian and Western European scholars deciphered Urartian writing and read Urartian rock inscriptions. The central regions of Urartu, lying in the present-day territory of Turkey, were explored by several expeditions, including one from Russia, which worked there at the time of World War I. The Orientalist Iosif Orbeli, later Director of the Hermitage, took part in this work. In the 1920s and '30s, active search for Urartian antiquities was started in Transcaucasia. A strong need was felt to obtain basic archaeological materials to supplement the data of written sources. In 1939, after years of exploration and careful deliberation, excavations on the Karmir-Blur hill were at last begun.

The results surpassed all expectations. The fortress had been quickly destroyed by fire, and the ruins preserved much telling evidence of its last hours: skeletons of people and animals overtaken by sudden death — even remains of a toad who sought for refuge among the cool shadows of a huge wine storehouse. Some flowers in a tuft of grass indicated the time of the attack: the earlier half of August. The hoards of hastily hidden valuables, the stored foodstuffs that had served no one's need, the charred heaps of grain, and even a loaf of baked bread, enabled the archaeologists to visualize the way of life and the picture of the fall of the Urartian outpost. The very suddenness of its destruction was a factor conducive to the preservation of a multitude of archaeological objects, including an exceptionally rich assortment of pottery, from household utensils to art works; ritual shields and helmets with decorative designs and inscriptions; minor sculpture; details of horse's harness;

clay tablets covered with writing; women's ornaments; in a word, objects representing every aspect of Urartian life.

The results of the excavations provided ample materials for many years of historical study. The Armenian government gave to the Hermitage a representative collection of Karmir-Blur finds. Today the Urartu Room contains, side by side with the lovely details from a throne, placed there in the 19th century, the shields, swords, quivers, various vessels, personal ornaments, recovered by the efforts of Hermitage archaeologists.

A place of honour in the annals of world archaeology belongs to a collection of finds from the Moshchevaya Balka burial ground in the North Caucasus, a territory identified as part of the Great Silk Route. Situated on a terrace stretching along the side of a sandstone slope, the burial ground presented exceptionally favourable conditions for the conservation of the grave goods over the centuries. The dry soil and the pure mountain air have preserved undamaged beautiful examples of textile goods — early medieval patterned silks, decorated with brightly coloured ornamental motifs and figurative subjects and made into clothes. The finds include whole articles of costume and even entire sets for men's, women's, and children's wear. The tombs, discovered by mere chance, were thoroughly investigated by the Hermitage expeditions of the early 1970s. They contained burials of local tribesmen, including, in all probability, some of the chiefs and nobles. The magnificent silks, valued in those days above the price of gold, were the tribute exacted by local tribes from caravan owners for traversing their land on the way westward. Owing to this practice, the Hermitage has at its disposal a unique complex of most rare fabrics. The Hermitage can boast of a collection unparalleled for its wealth; other world museums possess only fragments of such silks. Their beauty speaks for itself, making it clear why they were valued so highly as to be well worth carrying to distant countries as objects of foreign trade.

It was in the 20th century that historical research in the sphere of Russian culture took a particularly active form in the Hermitage. Archaeological and ethnographic field work assumed a place of great significance. From the 1950s on, numerous important finds were added to the Museum collections. Hermitage expeditions to out-of-the-way, forgotten villages of the Russian North have been collecting in the course of several decades hundreds of objects of applied art, icons, and early printed books, and thereby saving them from destruction.

Special attention was given to monuments of Old Russian architecture in the main centres of its flowering. The results of Hermitage expeditions threw a new light on many problems in the history of Russian architecture. Particularly remarkable success was achieved by the expedition working at Pskov. For 40 years Hermitage archaeologists, in collaboration with their Pskovian colleagues, conducted systematic diggings of the site of the so-called Dovmont City, one of the central areas of the town. The works were directed first by Grigory Grozdilov and later by Vasily Beletsky.

The diggings helped to reconstruct the history of the city's growth, to trace the functional evolution of its various parts, and to reveal the planning of its ancient streets and roads. The excavation site turned into an open-air museum and became one of remarkable landmarks of Pskov. The highest point of the exploration was reached with the discovery of several church buildings dating from the 13th to the 15th centuries; in some of them, 14th-century frescoes had survived. Fragments of splendid Pskovian murals entered the Hermitage collection, adding much to our knowledge of the specific features of the local school of painting and its links with other countries.

Credit for these discoveries must go not only to the archaeologists but also to the Museum's restorers of mural paintings. They developed new methods for the conservation of Pskovian frescoes, as they had done some time before for the murals of Pianjikent.

The early years of the 20th century were marked by great discoveries in Central Asia, where Russian and Western European scholars seemed to vie with one another in exploring for the remains of forgotten ancient cultures.

One of the most remarkable sites was a Buddhist cave

*Pianjikent. Archaeological
excavations. Photograph*

monastery near Tun-huang, at China's western border, where the Great Silk Route took its beginning. The walls of its numerous caves were painted with brilliantly coloured pictures of personages of the Buddhist pantheon, which gave to this shrine its name of the Caves of a Thousand Buddhas. The caves also contained beautiful sculptures, pictures painted on silk, and a monastery library.

Famous Oriental scholars from different countries, among them Sir Aurel Stein of England, and Paul Pelliot of France, enriched the museums of their lands with relics from Tun-huang. Russian archaeologists, too, joined in the race. Two expeditions went to Chinese Turkestan. They were directed by Sergei Oldenburg, one of the world's best specialists in Buddhism, a prominent student of Indian and Central Asian cultures, and a brilliant philologist and folklorist. He added to his academic endowments an organizing ability and experience in directing archaeological work. This ensured the success of his expeditions to the desert and helped in his later life, especially after the 1917 revolution, to do much for the preservation of all that was best in Russian science: Oldenburg was Permanent Secretary of the Academy of Sciences.*

The Oldenburg expedition of 1909–10 discovered several ancient oases cities among the desert. The sites contained some cave shrines with wall paintings in them. The finds included large and small sculpture, a great part of it vividly coloured. All these finds were datable to the 10th and 11th centuries. In 1914–15, the expedition reached Tun-huang. Here its work was interrupted by World War I. Nevertheless, collections of wonderful fragments of Buddhist murals, as well as those of sculptures, painted silks, manuscript and printed books, were eventually brought to Petrograd without any losses.

The Tun-huang collections changed their whereabouts several times passing on from one scientific body to another. In the late 1920s, the part containing art works was trans-

* The author wishes to express his gratitude to Kira Samosiuk of the Hermitage Oriental Department for drawing his attention to relevant materials in the collections under her curatorship.

ferred to the Hermitage. Here they formed a section of the Museum's Oriental Department, illustrating the cultural achievements of China and the neighbouring states from the mid-4th to the 14th centuries, but mainly those of the brilliant reign of the T'ang dynasty (7th–10th centuries). The collections of texts, also brought from Tun-huang, are now in the Academy of Sciences Institute for Oriental Studies.

The practice of removing and exporting ancient relics from their original environment where, although lost and forgotten, they had survived for centuries, may be condemned from the point of view of our present-day ethics. Still, there was a positive side to it that must not be overlooked. Firstly, it was precisely through museum research and library work of several generations of European scholars that these materials have served to reconstruct the picture of the cultures they represented and come to be appreciated the world over. Secondly, it may be safely inferred that many of these cultural treasures would have perished in the vortex of historical upheavals of our age — from which no country and no region were immune — had they not found a haven of peace within museum walls.

Asiatic travels of exploration, full of danger but rich in discoveries, appealed to many men of strong individuality. Piotr Kozlov, a pupil and companion of the great explorer Nikolai Przewalski, was one of this class of men. His travels across the immense expanses of the severe and inhospitable regions of Mongolia and Tibet led to the discovery of the Dead City of Khara-Khoto, lost among the sands of the desert of Gobi. These were the ruins of a town once inhabited by the Tangut, a forgotten people, who, in the Middle Ages, built a state called Si Hia. A neighbour of China, Si Hia flourished, and rivalry arose between two states. The Tangut city was repeatedly attacked, destroyed, and rebuilt. Its final collapse came in the 13th century, when habitation of the site ceased, and it was buried under the sands of the desert. Legends of the Dead City, current among the dwellers of the region, scraps of knowledge accidentally picked up, and — lastly — his explorer's intuition, led Kozlov to Khara-Khoto in 1908–9. There he excavated a Buddhist ceremonial structure where, in accordance with the local custom, the dead were laid with ritual objects for grave gods: books and icons. It was not before 1920 that Kozlov was able to come to Khara-Khoto for a second time, and resume his excavations which yielded extremely important results. Regrettably, in the interim the place had been visited by the ubiquitous Sir Aurel Stein.

The dry climate of the desert ensured excellent preservation of the finds — numerous examples of Tibeto-Tangut and Chinese painting on paper, on silk, and on canvas, along with a whole library of Tangut books. Several generations of Orientalists who studied these materials succeeded finally in deciphering the Tangut script and learning the language. A wealth of information on the history, culture, and way of life of a people long gone was revealed. The Khara-Khoto art works, primarily the marvellous religious paintings on silk and canvas, together with the beautiful sculptures transferred to the Hermitage in 1933 from the Russian Museum, made the Hermitage collection famous as one of the world's greatest treasuries of Buddhist art.

Other finds brought back by Kozlov also entered the Museum. They included a splendid assemblage of ancient and medieval textiles and specimens of appliqué work on felt from the burials of Hun chieftains in the mountains of Noin Ula, Mongolia.

Over a long period of time, Central Asia, was an object of active archaeological exploration and research. Hermitage archaeologists were also involved in this work, which resulted in the discovery of numerous ancient sites.

One of the most remarkable discoveries was associated with the history of the Sogdian state. In the early medieval times, it occupied the plains and mountains of Western Central Asia, approximately in the area of modern Samarkand. In 1932, a shepherd tending his flock on the flat top of the Mug Mountain in the upper reaches of the Zeravshan, stumbled on a wicker basket containing ancient manuscripts. The language of these documents was found, on investigation, to be Sogdian. The site was excavated under the direction of Leningrad archaeologists. They unearthed the remains of a medieval castle where, alongside a multitude of objects of daily use, weapons, and a painted shield, was found a whole archive of documents. The study of the documents, one of which was in Arabic, showed that the castle belonged to the Sogdian prince Divastich, the lord of the city of Pianjikent, who took refuge in the stronghold during the Arab conquest of the region in the late 7th century. The manuscripts contained much information concerning the Sogdians' life and culture, and some data on their prince, Divastich.

In 1946, excavations were started on the site of Pianjikent, Divastich's city situated on the plain. At different times, the expedition was directed by Alexander Yakubovsky, Mikhail Dyakonov, Alexander Belenitsky, and Boris Marshak. The diggings, which took many field seasons, revealed a standard pattern of a medieval town with its citadel, its palaces, dwelling houses, temples, artisans' workshops, and dealers' shops. But the most remarkable feature which made Pianjikent famous all over the world, were its fresco paintings, showing figures of deities and mythological and everyday scenes. For decades, Hermitage archaeologists, together with their local colleagues, worked on the Pianjikent site. All the while Hermitage restorers were engaged in fixing and restoring the murals. Now some of the frescoes form part of the permanent exposition in the Hermitage rooms, where they are accompanied by wooden sculptures which had escaped destruction during the conflagration owing to a layer of charcoal formed on their surface.

During the post-revolutionary period, active archaeological work was one of the main sources of new accessions to the Museum, its results being — to a certain extent — comparable to those achieved by the Emperors' passionate collecting. The names of archaeological sites — Pazyryk, Pianjikent, Karmir-Blur — are as meaningful to the art lover as are those of the great private collectors: Crozat, Walpole, Brühl, Shchukin, or Morozov.

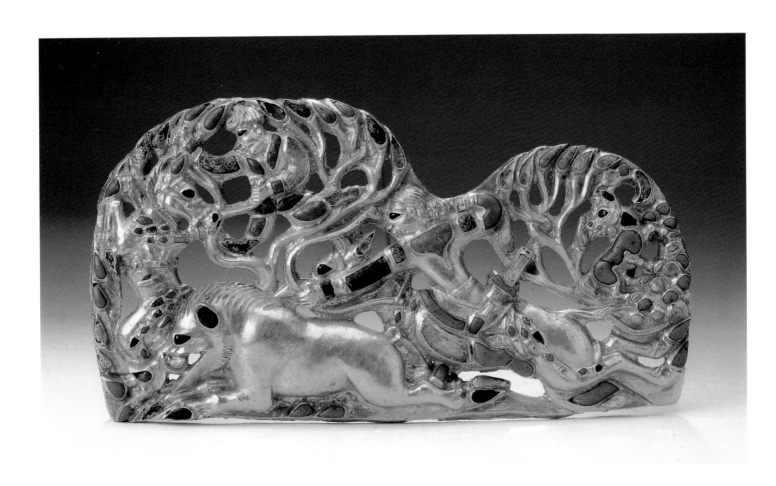

*Belt plaque: Hunting in the Forest.
4th–3rd centuries B.C. Sakaean
culture. Gold. Length 19.5 cm.
The Hermitage. From the Siberian
collection of Peter the Great. 1716*

*Aigrette. 5th–4th centuries B.C. Iran.
Gold. Height 15.4 cm. The Hermitage.
From the Siberian collection of Peter
the Great. 1716*

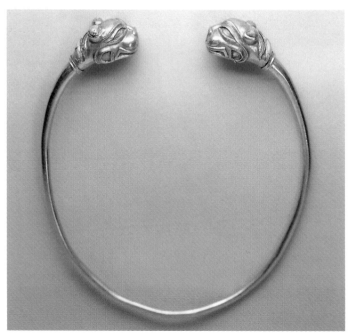

Belt plaque: The Tree of Life.
4th–3rd centuries B.C. Gold. Length
15.5 cm. The Hermitage. From the
Siberian collection of Peter the Great.
1716

Torque (grivna) decorated with lions'
heads. 4th century B.C. Iran. Gold.
Diam. 18.5 cm. The Hermitage. From
the Siberian collection of Peter the
Great. 1716

213

Finial shaped as a gryphon with a stag's head in its beak. 5th century B.C. Scythian epoch. Wood, leather. Height 27 cm. The Hermitage. From the Pazyryk Barrow II

Chariot. 5th–4th centuries B.C. Height 300 cm. The Hermitage. From the Pazyryk Barrow V

The excavations of Scythian barrows at Pazyryk in the Altai mountains, South Siberia, led to sensational discoveries. Preserved in the permanent frost layer were the most ancient objects ever found: a dismantled wagon, felt rugs and various utensils produced by the nomads nearly twenty-five hundred years ago.

Pile carpet. 5th–4th centuries B.C.
183 × 200 cm. The Hermitage. From
the Pazyryk Barrow V

Fragments of a felt rug. 5th–4th centuries B.C. The Hermitage. From the Pazyryk Barrow V

217

Bowls. 8th century B.C. Urartu.
Bronze. Diam. 19.5 cm. The Hermitage.
From Karmir-Blur

Archaeological excavations on the territo-
ry of the most ancient state in Transcau-
casia yielded a number of important
finds, among them a bronze figurine of
an Urartian deity, Chaldis (fragment
of a throne), bowls, a helmet and a shield
with inscriptions and representations of
Urartian rulers.

218

A winged lion with a human torso. Fragment of a throne. 8th century B.C. Urartu. Bronze. Height 16 cm. The Hermitage. From Toprakh-Kale. 1885

Shield of King Sarduris. 8th century B.C. Urartu. Bronze. Diam. approx. 70 cm. The Hermitage. From Karmir-Blur

Helmet of King Sarduris. 8th century B.C. Urartu. Bronze. Height approx. 20 cm; diam. 23 cm. The Hermitage. From Karmir-Blur

Vessel: Scythian Warriors. 4th century B.C. Greece. Electrum. Height 13 cm. The Hermitage. From Kul-Oba. 1831

The findings of Kul-Oba provide a striking picture of the convergence of Hellenic and Scythian cultures.

219

220

221

*Panther. Late 7th century B.C.
Scythian epoch. Gold. Length
32.6 cm. The Hermitage. From the
Kelermes Barrow. 1903*

*The Hermitage possesses the most com-
prehensive collection of Scythian art in
the world. Here you can see a fine speci-
men of the Scythian "animal style" —
a gold figurine of a panther.*

*Pendant. 4th century B.C. Greece.
Gold. Height 9.5 cm. The Hermitage.
From Kul-Oba. 1831*

*Temple pendant with the head of
Athena. 4th century B.C. Greece.
Gold. Length 17.5 cm. The Hermit-
age. From Kul-Oba. 1831*

*Comb. Late 5th – early 4th cen-
turies B.C. Scythian epoch. Gold.
Height 12.3 cm. The Hermitage.
From the Solokha Barrow. 1913*

*Chertomlyk vase. 4th century B.C.
Silver. Height 70 cm. The Hermitage.
From the Chertomlyk Barrow. 1863*

*One of the most celebrated treasures of
the Hermitage is the Chertomlyk vase —
a silver vessel, which probably used to
contain mare's milk. It is decorated with
applied vegetative and animal motifs
as well as reliefs depicting Scythian
warriors.*

*Phial. 4th century B.C.
Hellenic-Scythian period. Gold.
Diam. 21.8 cm. The Hermitage.
From the Solokha Barrow. 1913*

*Torque (grivna) with figures of
horsemen. 4th century B.C.
Hellenic-Scythian period. Gold.
Length 77.5 cm. The Hermitage.
From Kul-Oba. 1831*

Sgraffito picture of the ship "Isis".
3rd century B.C. Nymphaeum. Length
of ship 120 cm. The Hermitage. From
Nymphaeum. 1982

226

One of the most significant discoveries made at Nymphaeum is a fresco with numerous scratched contours of ships and inscriptions, found in 1982. Particularly interesting is the large sgraffito picture of the ship "Isis" which arrived at the Black Sea coast from Alexandria. A citizen of Nymphaeum, as far back as the 3rd century B.C., recorded his impression of this unusual foreign vessel.

227

*Plate. Bahram-Gur and Azadeh
Hunting. Late 6th – first half of
the 7th century. Iran. Silver. Diam.
21.7 cm. The Hermitage. Found in
Viatka Province. 1927*

*Plate: Goddess Riding a Dragon.
First half of the 7th century. Iran.
Silver. Diam. 22.2 cm. The Hermit-
age. Found in Viatka Province. 1927*

*The Hermitage boasts a unique collec-
tion of Sassanian gold- and silverware,
including ornaments and signs of royal
distinction, tableware and valuable
gifts. Together they present a gallery of
Sassanian rulers, noblemen, and various
symbols and spirits of the Zoroastrian
pantheon.*

228

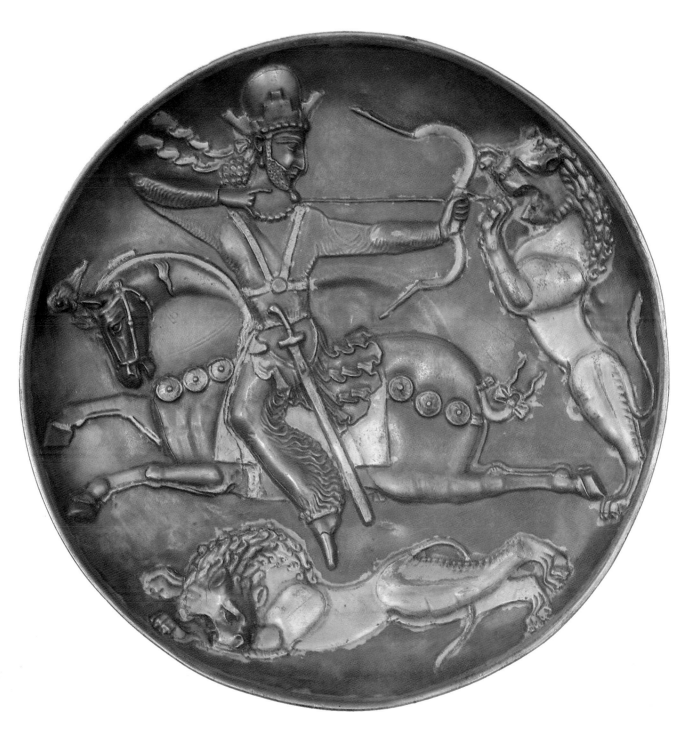

Plate: King Shapur II Hunting.
4th century. Iran. Silver. Diam.
22.9 cm. The Hermitage. Found
in Viatka Province. 1927

*Fragment of silk fabric: Bahram-Gur
Hunting. 8th century. Byzantium.
99 × 90 cm. The Hermitage. Found in
Moshchevaya Balka*

*Favourable environmental conditions in
the Moshchevaya Balka burial ground
in the North Caucasus, a territory
which formed part of the Great Silk
Route, helped to preserve undamaged
beautiful examples of textiles dating
from the 8th and 9th centuries.*

*Silk amulet bag. 9th century.
Byzantium. 11 × 8 cm. The Hermitage. Found in Moshchevaya Balka*

*Fresco: A Youth and a Girl on
Horseback. Central Asia. Pianjikent.
113 × 95 cm. The Hermitage. Found
by a Tajik archaeological expedition*

*The most remarkable feature which
made Pianjikent famous all over the
world are its fresco paintings decorating
the walls in the houses of eminent
townsmen. One of them illustrates a literary subject and shows a youth and a
girl on horseback.*

Fresco: Saint Martyrs.
Mid-14th century. Pskov.
182 × 132 cm. The Hermitage

Fresco: A Saint. 15th century. Pskov.
18.3 × 16.2 cm. The Hermitage

Pskovian murals discovered in the course of archaeological excavations opened a new page in the history of Old Russian fresco painting.

Temple pendant (kolt). 12th–13th centuries. Kiev. Gold, enamel. 5.5 × 5.6 cm. The Hermitage. From the Archaeological Commission. 1888

Unknown goldsmiths of the pre-Mongolian Rus created head ornaments of unsurpassed beauty and artistry. Temple pendants, or kolts, were the most attractive elements in a female headdress.

232

233

Buddha. 9th century. Bezeklik-Turfan. Clay. Height 101 cm. The Hermitage. Found by the First Sergei Oldenburg Expedition to Turkestan. 1909–10

Shown here are monuments of Buddhist art from the East Turkestan (now one of Chinese provinces) dating from the mid-9th to 13th century.

Horseman. 7th–10th centuries. Turfan. Clay. Height 26 cm. The Hermitage. Found by the First Sergei Oldenburg Expedition to Turkestan. 1909–10

Two-headed Buddha. 12th–13th centuries. Khara-Khoto. Clay. Height 62 cm. The Hermitage. Found by the Piotr Kozlov expedition. 1909

Here we see specimens of Buddhist art found in the Dead City of Khara-Khoto, a town once inhabited by the Tangut, a forgotten people who built, between the 10th and 13th centuries, a state called Si Hia (now one of Chinese provinces).

Figures of monks and bodhisattvas. Fragment of a wall painting in the Buddhist temple. 9th century. Shikshin. 92 × 104 cm. The Hermitage. Found by the First Sergei Oldenburg Expedition to Turkestan. 1909–10

Bodhisattva. Fragment of a wall painting in the Buddhist temple. 8th–9th centuries. 30 × 38 cm. The Hermitage. Found by the First Sergei Oldenburg Expedition to Turkestan. 1909–10

Silk scroll: Planet Deity. 11th century. Khara-Khoto. 102 × 66 cm. The Hermitage

Tangka: Eleven-faced and Eight-armed Avalokitesvara. 12th century. Khara-Khoto. Canvas. 132 × 94 cm. The Hermitage

236

INDEX OF ILLUSTRATIONS
(IN AN ALPHABETICAL ORDER, WITH NUMBERS REFERING TO PAGES)

Oleg Neverov, Mikhail Piotrovsky

THE HERMITAGE
Essays on the History of the Collection

Text in English

Slavia. St Petersburg. 1997
Computer-aided makeup by the MEGAS design bureau. St Petersburg
Produced and printed by P&CS, Milan, Italy